Regulating Pensions:

Too Many Rules,
Too Little Competition?

DAVID SIMPSON

Economic Adviser,
The Standard Life Assurance Company

Published by
INSTITUTE OF ECONOMIC AFFAIRS
1996

First published in November 1996

by

THE INSTITUTE OF ECONOMIC AFFAIRS
2 Lord North Street, Westminster,
London SW1P 3LB

Hobart Paper 131

ISSN 0073-2818

ISBN 0-255 36389-3

Printed in Great Britain by
HARTINGTON FINE ARTS LIMITED
Marlborough Road, Churchill Industrial Estate,
Lancing, W. Sussex
Set in Baskerville Roman 11 on 12 point

CONTENTS

[3]

[4]

[5]

FOREWORD

Financial services provided to individuals are generally regarded as prime targets for regulation. It is claimed that consumers lack information about such infrequently purchased and complex products as pensions, endowments, unit trusts and similar long-term investments. Moreover, the suitability of these products for particular individuals may only become clear many years after their purchase.

Markets for such services are, it is said, 'imperfect' and subject to 'failures'. Many economists invoke the so-called 'lemons' problem: in a market with uncertainty about quality, where buyers have difficulty distinguishing good from bad products, there may be a general distrust of sellers, quality may tend to be depressed and business may decline. So, it is argued, competitive markets in financial services are not capable of protecting consumers. Regulation is required if properly informed decisions are to be made.

In Hobart Paper 131, Professor David Simpson – who is economic adviser to Standard Life, and an Honorary Professor at Heriot-Watt University – challenges some of these propositions about the need to regulate markets for long-term personal investments, points to serious regulatory failures and recommends numerous changes to the regulatory régime. Though his detailed recommendations refer to Britain, his criticisms of financial services regulation and the changes he suggests have a wider applicability, in particular to the debate on this subject which is just beginning in Europe.

He begins, in Section II, by reviewing the arguments of principle used by supporters of regulation which relate mainly to various sources of imperfection and failure. He then explains (Section III) the origins of the present system of financial regulation in Britain: the Financial Services Act of 1986 followed the Gower Report and established, *inter alia*, a Personal Investment Authority to regulate the types of investments with which he is concerned.

Professor Simpson argues in Sections IV, V and VI that the Act has failed. It created a 'multi-tiered bureaucracy' which lays down detailed procedures to be followed in dealing with customers, what information they should receive and what can and cannot be sold to them. Compliance costs may amount to around 9 per cent of industry turnover. Nevertheless, the act has failed to protect investors and it has led to a reduced rate of innovation and a loss of confidence in the industry. Regulatory objectives have been confused, over-prescriptive procedures have been used, and the regulatory bodies have lacked accountability.

The answer, he argues, is a new approach which works with market forces rather than trying to oppose them. Competition has been increasing (Section VII), despite the constraints of regulation, as a result of new entrants to the industry. Corporate branding – which '...is a natural response of competitive markets to the customer need for confidence' – has been emphasised as companies such as Virgin, Direct Line, Marks & Spencer and the big banks have entered the market. Prices have been falling and service standards have increased as a result of increased competition.

Under the new approach which Professor Simpson favours (Sections VIII and IX), instead of prescriptive regulation there would be promotion of '...vigorous competition accompanied by the effective enforcement of laws against fraud and unfair trading'. Instead of '...laying off the task of being honest to an outside inspector', companies would be obliged to recognise that a '...reputation for trustworthiness is a competitive asset in the personal investment market'. Effective competition would promote integrity. Markets, freed from detailed regulation, would develop solutions to the problem of advice – such as its separation from the supply of products, and knowledge-based computer software for financial planning.

Instead of the paternalistic objective of 'consumer protection', Professor Simpson would like to see regulation dedicated to the creation of a market in which '...consumers can deal with confidence'. Companies would work within a code of conduct, enforceable at law, much of which can be derived from existing laws against misrepresentation. The 'multi-tiered bureaucracy' would be replaced by a single regulatory body for the marketing of all personal financial services which would monitor compliance with the code of conduct, promote comparative performance data and organise a programme of consumer financial planning awareness.

Radical solutions, such as those advocated by Professor Simpson, will not appeal to everyone. They will appear unattractive to those who favour detailed regulation because they do not appreciate that markets are the most effective devices so far evolved to provide information and stimulate innovation. Nor will they appeal to all parts of the financial services industry since the present regulatory régime is a protective barrier which some incumbents may welcome. But his case is sufficiently clear and detailed that it ought to provoke a new, fundamental examination of the relative virtues of competition and prescriptive regulation in retail financial markets.

The views expressed in Hobart Paper 131 are intended to stimulate debate on this important issue at a time when financial regulation is under review by government and regulators, both in Britain and in other countries. As in all Institute publications, the views are those of the author, not of the IEA (which has no corporate view), its Trustees, Directors or Advisers.

November 1996　　　　　　　　　COLIN ROBINSON
Editorial Director, Institute of Economic Affairs;
Professor of Economics, University of Surrey

THE AUTHOR

DAVID SIMPSON was educated at the Universities of Edinburgh and Harvard, and then worked for the Statistical Office of the United Nations in New York. From 1975 to 1988 he was Professor of Economics at the University of Strathclyde. He is now Economic Adviser to The Standard Life Assurance Company, an Honorary Professor at Heriot-Watt University, Edinburgh, and a member of the IEA's academic advisory council.

Professor Simpson's published writings include several books: *Problems of Input-Output Tables and Analysis* (1966); *General Equilibrium Analysis* (1975); and *The Political Economy of Growth* (1983); and articles in journals ranging from *Econometrica* to *Scientific American*. For the IEA, he wrote *The End of Macro Economics* (Hobart Paper No.126, 1994).

ACKNOWLEDGEMENTS

To a large degree, this paper is a development of ideas originated by Jim Stretton. However, neither he nor any of those other colleagues and friends who gave so generously of their time and knowledge in commenting on earlier drafts bears any responsibility for the views expressed here. Responsibility for those views, and for remaining errors and omissions, rests with the author alone.

I am especially indebted to Andrew Bomphrey of British American Financial Services, Scott Carswell, now retired from Standard Life, and Professor David Llewellyn of Loughborough University for their extensive comments. Very many others kindly responded to my requests for help. In particular, I would like to thank Martha Young for her diligent and enthusiastic research, and Joyce McMurdo for patiently producing an apparently interminable number of drafts.

D.S.

I. INTRODUCTION

There are at least two reasons why the regulation of the personal investment market should be a topic of widespread interest. *First* is its practical importance to every household. Decisions about long-term investment are perhaps the most important financial decisions which the great majority of people will ever make. For most people, the value of the funds from which they draw their retirement income will exceed the value of their house. Because of the one-off nature of the investment contract, the increasing proportion of the average lifetime spent in retirement, and the diminishing value of the basic state pension in relation to average earnings, the standard of living of most people in retirement will depend on getting their earlier investment decision right.

The *second* reason why the regulation of personal investment is an important issue is that it represents a case study in the ineffectiveness of regulation. Experience of the long-term personal investment market in the UK over the past 10 years has demonstrated that, on the whole, regulation does not work while competition does.

Since the privatisation of the major utilities, regulatory issues have featured prominently in the media. The regulation of personal investment, on the other hand, seems to have received less publicity. This seems strange since what is at stake in the case of the utilities is likely to be no more than a few hundred pounds on the annual electricity bill of the average household. In the case of personal investment, the choice between a suitable and unsuitable contract can mean a difference of thousands of pounds a year in post-retirement income.

The explanation lies in the difference between the regulatory problem in utilities and that in financial services. In the utilities, the problem for the regulator is to determine how the price of the product should be fixed: left to itself, the monopolistic market would be likely to produce a price higher than that which would be set in a competitive market. The rationale for regulatory intervention in utilities is that each of

[11]

the industries concerned is characterised by the existence of some degree of natural monopoly.

The problem in the long-term personal investment market is not one of monopoly. On the contrary, more than 200 companies are authorised by the DTI to transact life assurance business alone. The five largest of these companies account in total for less than 30 per cent of the market, a relatively low degree of concentration by the standards of other industries in the UK, and also by the standards of other European life assurance markets.[1] The problem in the long-term personal investment market is not monopoly but quality uncertainty. In this context the word 'quality' refers not only to the rate of return earned on the individual investment but to other characteristics of the investment contract, notably its suitability to the particular needs of the individual saver concerned. Not until very many years have elapsed, perhaps as many as 20 or 30, will the purchaser – or anyone else – be able to identify accurately the quality of the product. By that time, it is of course too late to make an alternative purchase.

Scope of the Paper

This *Hobart Paper* is concerned with those transactions in personal investment contracts which are regulated by the Personal Investment Authority (PIA).

Long-term personal investment services are a subset of financial services, formed by eliminating first of all wholesale financial services (transactions between firms) and concentrating on those financial services provided to individuals (that is, retail financial services), such as money transmission services, lending, borrowing, fund management and protection against risk. These services are typically provided by institutions such as banks, life and general insurance companies, fund management companies and intermediaries of various kinds. Historically, the providing companies have been subject to so-called prudential supervision by bodies which differed according to the type of institution. Thus the banks are supervised by the Bank of England, the insurance companies by the DTI, and so on. The purpose of this prudential regulation has been to ensure the

---

[1] G. Weidenfeld, 'The European Internal Insurance Market', in *Geneva Papers on Risk and Insurance*, No. 78, January 1996, p. 79.

solvency of the company supplying the financial service, thereby diminishing the risk of loss to consumers.

An additional, quite different, framework of regulation was introduced by the Financial Services Act of 1986 (FSA). Its purpose was to regulate the *marketing* of personal financial services, as opposed to their production, and it is this regulatory framework which is the subject of the present paper.

Under the FSA, the regulators are organised according to product category; the subset of the product range with which we are concerned excludes both deposit-taking and lending services (regulated by the Bank of England) and also the selling of securities such as equities and bonds through stockbrokers (regulated by the Securities and Futures Authority). What we are concerned with are sometimes called 'packaged' investment contracts, and are more familiarly recognised as being the types of investment contracts issued by life assurance companies, for example, pensions, endowment policies, unit trusts, PEPs and investment trusts. Amongst the products excluded from this regulatory régime are TESSAs (regulated by the Bank of England), and those risk protection contracts such as term assurance which have no investment element.

There are at least four sources of confusion about the boundaries of the regulated market. Similar contracts, for example, unit trusts, are provided by different institutions (banks, insurance companies, fund management companies). Within a class of similar contracts (for instance, long-term care), some may be regulated, others not. Contracts under one regulatory system may be close substitutes for those under another (guaranteed bonds). Finally, there are imports. Until 1994, a combination of regulation and taxation effectively prohibited any cross-border trade in personal investment contracts. Although discriminatory taxation continues to inhibit the development of such trade, the implementation of the Third Life Directive means that insurance companies authorised in other EU states may operate branches in the UK without requiring UK authorisation.

Thus the size of the regulated market is by no means clear. Matters are not helped by the relative neglect by the statistical authorities of financial services in favour of manufacturing. However, a rough idea of the size of the market may be determined from the following illustrative figures.

[13]

Around three-quarters of all households in the UK (over 17 million homes) have some form of long-term investment or protection contract. In 1994, the UK life insurance and pensions industry collected over £43 billion of premium income, and paid out around £30 billion to policyholders. Net sales of unit trusts to private investors amounted to £6 billion in the same year. The personal sector had a total of £995 billion invested in life and pensions funds at 31 December 1995.[2]

A professional economist addressing regulatory issues in the life assurance and pensions industry is faced with some difficulties of terminology. The usage of words in the profession and in the industry differs, with sometimes the one and sometimes the other being closer to common parlance. For example, it is normal in the industry, and indeed throughout the whole financial services sector, to refer to different types of personal savings contracts as 'products', to denote the act of purchasing such contracts as 'investment' and to use the word 'charges' to refer to the prices of contracts. Economists have their own terminology for these things which I have tried as far as possible to confine to Section II. In the rest of the paper, I have tried to adopt that usage which is likely to be best understood by those to whom this paper is addressed, namely the general reader who is neither an economist nor a practitioner.

The argument of the paper is presented as follows. Section II discusses some propositions in economic theory which are often invoked in support of regulatory intervention in the market for personal investment. As we shall see, considerations of economic theory were absent from the government papers which led up to the Financial Services Act. The third section describes the present regulatory system which was established by that Act, and the evidence of its failure is presented in Section IV. Reasons for the failure of the regulatory system are analysed in Section V. The costs of regulation are reviewed in Section VI. In Section VII, it is argued that effective competition only began in the industry in the early 1990s. In the short space of time which has elapsed since then, competition has succeeded in providing benefits to consumers where regulation has failed.

---

[2] Office of National Statistics (ONS), *Financial Statistics*, No. 409, London: HMSO, May 1996.

Proposals for regulatory reform are put forward in the eighth section. These are built around three principles: that vigorous competition accompanied by strict enforcement of the normal rules of fair trading provides the most effective form of consumer protection, that requiring buyers and sellers to follow certain prescribed procedures ('box ticking') is harmful to both parties, and that the regulatory authorities must be made more accountable for their actions. Section IX presents conclusions and recommendations. The argument of the whole paper is summarised in 10 points on the back cover.

Since this *Hobart Paper* is critical of the present system of regulation, and since the author is employed by a life assurance company, it might be supposed that the paper constitutes special pleading, and presents the industry's point of view. In fact, opinion in the industry is divided; many people in the industry have welcomed a prescriptive approach as it appears to offer regulatory certainty, and some want more of it.[3] The views expressed in this paper are personal, and do not represent either those of the industry or of the author's employer.

---

[3] See, for example, the response by the Association of British Insurers (ABI) to the Government's recent proposals on long-term care contracts.

II. THEORETICAL ARGUMENTS FOR REGULATORY INTERVENTION IN THE PERSONAL INVESTMENT MARKET

'The ultimate rationale of regulation designed to protect the consumer is to correct for market imperfections or market failure which would compromise consumer welfare in a regulation-free environment.' [1]

This is a statement which would be generally accepted by most mainstream or neo-classical economists. Non-economists should be warned, however, that in this context the terms 'market imperfection' and 'market failure' have quite specific meanings.

Market Failure

In contemporary economic debate, the presumption that competition is, in general, preferable to government intervention in the market-place, whether that intervention takes the form of regulation, taxation or subsidy, is usually underpinned by the neo-classical theory of value. Given a number of specific assumptions, this theory demonstrates logically that a system of competitive markets for goods and services will achieve what is called an 'efficient' allocation of resources. Through the process of voluntary exchange, mutually advantageous transactions will occur between sellers and buyers until no further transactions will benefit one party without causing disadvantage to the other. Such an allocation is said to be 'efficient'.

Amongst the many assumptions which underlie the neo-classical theory are that each individual participating in the market is assumed to be the best judge of his or her own interests, and to act consistently, maximising his utility (or personal satisfaction) within the constraints of the resources available to him. Consumer demand is autonomous (consumer sovereignty), and firms are assumed to attempt to

---

[1] D. T. Llewellyn, 'Regulation of Retail Investment Services', *Economic Affairs*, Vol. 15, No. 2, p.13.

maximise their profits. Other factors taken as given are the existing state of technology, the constancy of consumer tastes and preferences, and the existing distribution of assets.

Phenomena which must be absent if an efficient allocation of resources is to be realised by a system of competitive markets include monopolies, externalities, economies of scale and public goods (see below, note 5, p.18). A further assumption of the neo-classical model, which is critical to the present discussion, is that all participants in the market, both producers and consumers, *should have perfect knowledge of all opportunities which are open to them, both in the present and in the future.*

Many readers who are non-economists might think that these assumptions, when taken together, are so restrictive as to disqualify the neo-classical model from serious consideration as a guide to policy in the field of regulation of consumer markets. Nevertheless, the fact is that this has hitherto been the principal theoretical framework within which policy discussion has taken place, and we must therefore adhere to it for a little while longer.

Since all real-world markets are evidently imperfect in one or more of the senses specified, in particular with respect to information, it follows from the neo-classical model that government intervention in every market would appear to be justified. What guidance does the theory offer to the nature and extent of such intervention? The uncomfortable answer is none. There is a theory (the general theory of the second-best) which says that if an efficient allocation of resources is for any reason unattainable (for example, because of the existence of some imperfection which is not removable), then no general guidance can be offered as to what constitutes the second-best policy in the circumstances. In particular, observing the normal rules of efficiency in other markets (such as marginal cost pricing) will not necessarily be desirable.

Another limitation of the neo-classical theory is that it is static; it overlooks, for example, the harmful effects to consumers caused by the inhibiting effects of regulation on product and process innovation. Dynamic theories, on the other hand, recognise that costs to the whole economy are imposed when the adaptability of firms to their changing environment is reduced by regulatory intervention. Alternatives to the neo-classical approach to the analysis of market behaviour have been put forward. These include the Austrian[2] or market process theories, which emphasise the dynamic effects of competition, and the more pragmatic theories of 'workable competition'[3] and 'contestable mar-kets'.[4] Nevertheless, the neo-classical model continues to be the principal basis for discussion of policy in consumer protection.

Information Deficiencies as a Rationale for Regulation

The most obvious example of market imperfection or 'market failure' is the plain fact that in most markets for consumer goods or services market participants are far from perfectly informed. The criterion of market failure through a lack of perfect information might therefore, without further consideration, justify almost any intervention in consumer markets. Since this is a counsel of perfection, it is widely accepted that the appropriate goal ought to be 'adequate' rather than 'perfect' information. Information on price, quality and the terms of a contract permit buyers to make efficient choices in a market. Without adequate information, quasi-efficient choices cannot be made. With the wrong information, consumers will transmit the wrong signals to sellers about their preferred alternatives.

There are two general considerations which are important in understanding the rôle of inadequate information as a source of market failure. *First,* information has the properties of a 'public good'.[5] Since it is difficult for a person producing

---

2   I. M. Kirzner, *Competition and Entrepreneurship,* Chicago: University of Chicago Press, 1973.

3   F. M. Scherer, *Industrial Market Structure and Economic Performance,* Chicago: Rand McNally, 1980.

4   W. M. Baumol, J. C. Panzar and R. D. Willig, *Contestable Markets and the Theory of Industry Structure,* New York: Harcourt, Brace, Jovanovich, 1982.

5   This is another term with a specific meaning in economic theory. Public goods have nothing to do with public ownership. The two key properties of public goods are: (1) *Non-rivalness:* consumption of a unit of a public good by one individual does not diminish the availability of that good to be consumed by another individual; and (2) *Non-excludability:* it may be impossible (or very costly) to exclude particular individuals from the consumption of the good in question. If it is impossible to exclude those who would benefit from the consumption of a good but are unwilling to pay for it, it may not be possible to raise enough revenue to cover its cost of production. Thus the good may not

publicly available information to prevent non-paying customers from gaining access to it, there will be a tendency towards the under-provision of information, and therefore a shortage of well-informed consumers. For example, the type of research on product quality performed by the Consumers' Association may be provided in less than optimum amounts, because the results supplied to one consumer are ascertainable at negligible cost by others. Thus, the public good characteristic of information may provide a *prima facie* rationale for government subsidisation of the provision of certain kinds of consumer information, such as comparative analyses of the performance of different products.

Second, information has a 'market-perfecting' effect. This qualifies the previous conclusion, since it describes the fact that information need only be used by a small number of individuals in a market for suppliers to respond. Thus the marginal group of individuals who search for information and complain about defective products provides benefits to other consumers by keeping producers in line. It may therefore be argued that it is not necessary for all consumers to be well informed in order for markets to be behaving competitively.

Most analysis of the problems of information conducted within the framework of the neo-classical model proceeds under the supposition of a market for goods which are homogeneous in quality, but where consumers have imperfect information as to variations in *price*. In the stock market, for example, the principal concern of consumers (investors), and therefore of regulators, is price uncertainty. However, the problem of preventing the sale of unsuitable investment contracts to consumers is really about uncertainty as to the *quality* of the contract at the time of its purchase.

Long-term investment contracts such as pensions and endowments have some peculiar features:

- It is impossible for the consumer (or even the supplier) to know at the time of purchase the principal qualitative characteristic of the product, namely its future investment performance.

---

be produced at all or in insufficient quantity. Thus the market has failed. Examples of public goods include defence and research services.

- The duration of the contract rules out the possibility of the consumer gaining experience of the quality of the product through frequent purchase.

- By their nature, long-term personal savings contracts involve a continuing financial commitment.

- The value of the purchase as a proportion of the consumer's budget may be large, implying that a mistaken decision can have serious consequences.

- The consumer's uncertainty about the quality of the product, together with a lack of awareness of his needs, means he or she is largely reliant on the advice of the seller as to the *suitability* of the contract to those needs.

Each of these features can be found in another market. For example, the last is common to the markets for legal and medical services. But the long-term personal investment market may be unique in having all of these features in combination.

Economic theory would conclude that the long-term personal investment market is a market characterised by strong quality uncertainty.[6] Uncertainty exists about the quality of the investment performance of the contract, combined with uncertainty about the quality of the jointly supplied advice. (To the extent that charges may vary over the term of a contract, there will also be price uncertainty, but this is not an inherent feature of such contracts.)

Quality Uncertainty

In a celebrated article,[7] Akerlof addressed the problem of quality uncertainty, that is, the difficulty the consumer has in

---

[6] In general, consumers and other market participants do not have at their disposal either perfect knowledge or perfect foresight, as the neo-classical theory presumes. Instead, their knowledge of the range, quality and prices of the available goods or services is fragmentary and incomplete, perhaps even inaccurate. This type of uncertainty faced by market participants is not the kind to which a calculus of probability is applicable. It is more than just ignorance about the values that specific variables within a given problem structure will take on: it is a lack of complete knowledge about the very structure of the decision problem itself. More than that, not only is the structure of the decision problem unknown, but not all possible states of the world can be known.

[7] G. Akerlof, 'The Market for Lemons', *Quarterly Journal of Economics*, August 1970.

distinguishing good quality from bad quality products in certain markets. Akerlof showed that this could lead to general depression of quality below the level which would operate in a perfectly functioning market, with a resulting decline in the volume of business transacted. In the extreme case, no business at all might be transacted; here, there would be complete market failure.

This is the case where the average quality of a commodity supplied falls with the corresponding fall in the offer price. This problem arises because of asymmetric information: in the case of used cars (Akerlof's example), the seller has more or better information about quality than has the buyer.

In the case of a protection-type insurance contract, the circumstances can sometimes be reversed. The seller (the insurance company) is the party with the inadequate information. This then leads to what is known as adverse selection.[8] In the case of investment-type contracts, however, it is again the consumer who has access to inferior information about the quality of the products on offer. Of course, the supplier does not know with accuracy the likely future investment performance of the contract he is offering; nevertheless, he may have a better idea of its likely outcome than the would-be purchaser. However, since the quality of the contract on offer is unlikely to be correlated positively with the offer price, Akerlof's specific problem of acute market failure would not seem to arise in the context of the market for long-term investment contracts.

Despite this, quality uncertainty has been cited[9] as a justification for regulatory intervention in the contemporary UK market. It is argued that minimum quality standards should be imposed to remove inferior suppliers or inferior products or both from the market. Such measures might take the form of regulatory guarantees (deposit insurance), licensing of agents and suppliers (authorisation), or licensing of products (as formerly in Germany).

In fact, markets have evolved their own solutions to the problem of quality uncertainty. Such solutions include guar-

---

[8] With adverse selection, bad risks take out contracts while good risks do not, thus condemning the insurance company to the likelihood of loss.

[9] Llewellyn, *op.cit.*

antees offered by the seller, trade marks or branding, and seller's advertising.

So far as the last of these is concerned, there is of course the danger of the seller providing false or misleading information. This is perhaps the best known, most obvious and oldest reason for regulation. If a market is riddled with false claims, then consumers may lose confidence in the truth of *all* seller claims – that is, in the market as a whole. False or misleading claims ought to be of greatest concern in situations where consumers are unable to verify through experience the performance of the relevant quality attributes, for example in relation to relatively expensive and infrequently purchased products and in markets where sellers are not dependent on repeat purchases. In such markets, the provision of misleading information is often made a criminal offence (see Section VIII below).

If a seller is unconcerned about a potential customer as a 'repeat buyer', then he will have little incentive to provide him with accurate information or to disclose costs. Such a seller will invest his resources in overcoming consumer resistance, perhaps through aggressive sales tactics and false or misleading claims. The cold-calling life assurance salesman provides one such example. Conversely, house calls by industrial branch insurance salesmen provide in principle an opportunity for quality assurance to be established through the operation of a long-lasting customer/seller relationship.

Of course, claims are generally misleading rather than false. The problem with misleading claims is that they are often ambiguous, depending on consumers drawing incorrect inferences, and are consequently misleading to some but not to all consumers. However, a programme of regulation which is not sensitive to these facts and which seeks 'truth' at all costs may restrict unnecessarily the flow of market information. There may be reasons for protecting a minority of credulous consumers against misleading claims, but the costs of such a policy ought to be recognised.[10]

---

[10] More than 20 years after the enactment of the Trade Descriptions Act, it still remains unclear who is to be protected – the reasonable consumer or the credulous consumer. (See I. D. C. Ramsay, *Rationales for Intervention in the Consumer Marketplace*, London: Office of Fair Trading, Occasional Paper, December 1984.)

Quality of Advice

Regulating product quality alone may be ineffective where the question of suitability arises. A product may be of high quality in all respects, but it may not be suitable for a particular consumer's needs. This problem is particularly acute where the supply of a product or service and advice about the quality of the service are jointly provided, for example in the case of the supply of legal and medical services and in the selling of investment contracts through intermediaries. A consumer may have difficulty in judging the quality of the advice, and whether the service is necessary. This joint supply problem may be particularly acute with those services which are purchased infrequently, and where there may be significant asymmetry in the information available to seller and consumer. It is this problem which is a major justification for the fiduciary duty of solicitors to their clients. The economic assumption of self-interested behaviour suggests, however, that there may be inappropriate levels of quality of advice in some investment markets (commission bias). Even after the service has been performed, a consumer may be unsure as to whether the particular level of quality provided matches his needs.

Furthermore, actual experience of a product or service may not reveal clearly either performance deficiencies or the nature of these deficiencies. For example, in the installation of home insulation it may be difficult for the consumer to know whether subsequent performance deficiencies are attributable to the insulation or to the installation. Consumers buying infrequently purchased products or services may also have difficulty in estimating post-purchase costs over the life-cycle of the product or service.

Because of this lack of knowledge, consumers may be unable to act on their dissatisfaction, either by altering their behaviour or by informing third parties. Consumer complaints may be flawed, therefore, as a guide to those markets most in need of intervention. For example, consumer complaints concerning legal or medical services, particularly in those areas where relatively unsophisticated consumers infrequently purchase services, are probably not a very accurate indicator of the nature of the real problems in these markets. Individuals are often unable to evaluate accurately the quality of the services performed except through superficial signals, for example, delays or inattention.

The Principal-Agent Problem

The consumer's uncertainty about product quality and the quality of advice can be regarded as an aspect of what economists call the principal-agent problem. Such a problem is said to arise whenever there is imperfect information about what action an agent has undertaken or should undertake on behalf of his principal.

Even where the principal (the consumer) can observe the action taken by his agent (the selling agent), the principal cannot know whether the agent took the action he himself would have taken in the given circumstances, because the agent acts on information different from that available to the principal.

Since, in general, the pay-offs to agents will differ from those to the principal, the agent will not, in general, take the action which the principal would like him to take or that he would have taken in the presence of perfect information.

It is sometimes suggested that a regulatory body can enjoy economies of scale in monitoring on behalf of consumers the actions of their agents, and that this provides a rationale for excluding from the market those agents who habitually provide bad advice. The difficulty, of course, remains the subjectivity of judgements about the quality of advice.

Bounded Rationality

The idea of bounded rationality[11] recognises that individuals are only able to receive, store and process a limited amount of information. In facing complex decisions they tend therefore to simplify the problem and to reduce the number of alternatives. Observation has suggested some general principles concerning the types of strategies used by individuals to process information. Four of these strategies may be relevant here.

* *First,* individuals will tend to use more readily available and vivid information, limited to a small number of alternatives, even though a larger number is available. This underlines the importance of personal selling and point-of-sale information. It also suggests that where product information is required to be disclosed to a consumer, it

---

[11] H. A. Simon, *Models of Bounded Rationality,* Cambridge, Mass.: MIT Press, 1982.

should be limited in quantity, should be understandable and should concentrate on the purpose of the product.

- *Second,* consumers, when searching for new products or information will refer initially to previous experience.

- *Third,* individuals may prefer anecdotal information to statistical data on product quality.

- *Fourth,* bounded rationality indicates that consumer search tends to be limited to a small number of alternatives.

The Theory of Public Choice

Until the early 1960s, economists believed, or affected to believe, that government regulation of markets was an altruistic activity undertaken with the exclusive purpose of benefiting the general public, and that this represented an adequate response to various kinds of market failure. Legislators, regulators, and administrators were all implicitly assumed to be disinterested maximisers of the social welfare, and any costs imposed by regulation on the economy were thought to be associated entirely with achieving some well-defined social objective. Then came the *theory of public choice*,[12] which applied the methods of economic analysis to the traditional questions of political science. According to this theory, legislators and civil servants are moved by considerations of self-interest just as much as are businessmen. Legislators can be expected to vote in their legislature for policies which will help to get them re-elected. Just as managers in General Motors are assumed to be trying to design and sell good cars because that is how promotions and pay rises are secured, so it is assumed in the theory of public choice that civil servants will be attempting to produce policies which in the eyes of their superiors are good, because that is how their promotion and pay rises are secured.

However, the attenuation of control characteristic of all bureaucracies means that much of what is done by lower-ranking officials is simply unknown to those of higher rank. This provides civil servants with the opportunity to pursue

---

[12] J.M. Buchanan and G. Tullock, *The Calculus of Consent: Logical Foundations of Constitutional Democracy,* Ann Arbor: University of Michigan Press, 1962.

their private agendas which frequently include expanding the size of their own departments.

The Economic Theory of Regulation

Building on the theory of public choice, Stigler attempted for the first time to offer a theory of the regulatory process.[13] According to Stigler, the central tasks of a theory of regulation are to explain who will receive the benefits and who will bear the costs of regulation, what form regulation will take, and what the effects of regulation will be on the allocation of resources. In this view, regulation represents the pursuit of regulatory rents through competition for coercive transfers of wealth in the political market-place.

Not only does regulation re-allocate wealth, its other significant economic consequence is that it imposes dead-weight costs on the economy. The review, monitoring and other bureaucratic procedures of various types significantly increase the transaction costs associated with change in response to new conditions. In a democracy, the public choice problems associated with majority rule tend to produce regulatory outcomes which are often inefficient and wasteful.

By rejecting the traditional approach of treating public policy as a mixture of benevolent public interest and unintentional blunders, the theory of regulation, which began with Stigler's article, has alerted observers to the political usefulness of apparently inefficient policies. While it is occasionally acknowledged by regulators[14] that they may pursue their own aims so as to maximise personal objectives such as career development and political influence, most of the discussion of the regulation of financial markets in the UK still continues to be conducted on the pre-1962 assumption that all regulators and legislators are disinterested maximisers of the social welfare. In fact, recent developments in the theory of regulation suggest that the regulatory régime in force in any market at any given time represents an equilibrium in competition in the political market-place between opposing forces representing interest groups of various kinds, including the interests of politicians and of the

---

[13] G. Stigler, 'The Theory of Economic Regulation', *Bell Journal of Economics and Management Science*, Vol. 2, No. 1, 1971.

[14] Such as Llewellyn, *op.cit.*, p.2.

regulators themselves. It is not implied that this process of competition between pressure groups produces an outcome which is in any way optimal; simply that existing regulations reveal where marginal benefits equal marginal costs, somehow defined. Thus, one could attempt to explain the recent historical experience of de-regulation by saying that the regulation of particular industries tends to alter in cases where marginal benefits, marginal costs or both shift in relation to relevant interest groups on either side of the policy market.

III. THE PRESENT SYSTEM OF REGULATION

In July 1981, Professor L. C. B. Gower, a distinguished commercial lawyer, was invited by the then Secretary of State for Trade to review the existing framework of statutory protection for private and business investors in securities, and to make recommendations for new legislation.

Gower approached the task of preparing a new regulatory framework with the mindset of a corporate lawyer, apparently oblivious of the economic theory of regulation, with a political mandate that something must be seen to be done, and with some haste.[1] Government having adopted a policy of de-regulating the supply side of the financial services market, and at the same time wishing to shift the provision of the 'second pillar' of pensions from the state budget to the market, was easily stampeded by a number of minor scandals in the early 1980s. In 1980, Norton Warburg, an insurance broking and investment management firm, had collapsed with losses of £4 million. The company had invested clients' money in a number of unsound ventures. Amongst the many clients who lost money were retired staff of the Bank of England. Shortly thereafter, the commodities broker Doxford collapsed. Who nowadays has heard of Norton Warburg or Doxford? Gower reveals that, as long ago as 1939, civil servants had a scheme of statutory regulation for the personal investment market within which a fleet of self-regulatory bodies was to operate. Gower's rather similar scheme seems to have been put into effect without having been given the normal consideration which such a significant change should have enjoyed.

Gower did not pause to consider the relationship of regulation to the competitive market process, nor did he

---

[1] Since Gower received his commission in 1981, and the Financial Services Act did not come into effect until 1988, this may not seem like haste. But Gower effectively completed his Report by October 1983, and wrote then that 'I decided not to adopt the traditional time-consuming practice of inviting memoranda of evidence followed by formal oral hearings.' (L. C. B. Gower, *Review of Investor Protection, Part 1*, Cmnd.9125, London: HMSO, January 1984, para. 1.03.)

investigate the degree of competition in the industry for which he was to prescribe a régime of regulation. Had he done so, he might have come to the conclusion that the interests of investors would have been better served by measures to promote greater competition in the market than by introducing more regulation. He seems to have been unaware of contemporary government policy towards de-regulation in other industries. The result was that while the 1980s was for many industries, including wholesale financial markets, a period of de-regulation, for the retail financial markets it was a period of intensification of regulation.

Nowhere in Gower's two Reports nor in the 1985 White Paper is there any serious discussion of the objectives of regulation.[2] All that Gower had to say on the subject was that regulation 'should be no greater than is necessary to prevent reasonable people being made fools of'. However, implicit in these documents is the view that regulation is something which must necessarily work against market forces rather than with them.[3] The inference is implicit in the phrases 'consumer protection' and 'investor protection'. It is a misconception which still plagues present-day regulators.

The present system of regulation of the selling of personal investment services was established by the Financial Services Act of 1986. The FSA is concerned only with 'investments' and 'investment business'. Investments are defined to include shares and other securities, unit trusts and other schemes of collective investment, commodity and financial derivatives and most long-term life insurance contracts. They do not include tangible objects. Investment business is defined to include dealing in, managing and advising on investments. Investment business is distinguished from other financial services such as deposit-taking business covered by the Banking Act and the Building Societies Act and not regulated under the FSA.

The main responsibility for the operation of this system of regulation lies with the Securities and Investments Board (SIB), a non-governmental body exercising statutory powers transferred to it by the Treasury, and funded by levies on the industry.

---

[2] Part I, Cmnd.9125, January 1984; Part II, 1985; *Financial Services in the United Kingdom*, Cmnd.9432, January 1985.

[3] Gower, *op.cit.*, Part I, para. 1.16.

The SIB has declared that its main objectives in overseeing the regulation of investment business in the UK are:

1. To protect investors – especially private investors – for example, from firms conducting investment business fraudulently, from financially unsound investment firms and from unsuitable investment advice.

2. To promote clean and orderly investment markets – that is, markets which are free from abuse.

3. To guard against the failure of investment firms, and to mitigate the effects of any such failure.

While more than 23,000 firms are authorised to conduct investment business in the UK, most practical regulation is carried out by a number of specialist bodies, supervised by the SIB. These include three so-called self-regulating organisations (SROs), namely PIA, SFA and IMRO, nine recognised professional bodies (RPBs) and seven recognised investment exchanges (RIEs) (see Figure 1). Of the SROs, the Investment Management Regulatory Organisation (IMRO) regulates about 1,100 fund management firms, the Personal Investment Authority (PIA) regulates about 4,000 firms supplying or advising on contracts in life assurance and personal pensions, unit trusts and investment trust schemes. The Securities and Futures Authority (SFA) regulates about 1,300 firms involved in all the organised (mainly wholesale) city investment markets, such as the stock market.

The nine RPBs include the professional bodies for lawyers and accountants whose main activity is the practice of their profession, but who have some minor involvement in investment business.

SIB also supervises the seven UK RIEs, including the London Stock Exchange and the London International Financial Futures and Options Exchange (LIFFE).

Within this framework there have always been anomalies and overlaps. For example, while the PIA is responsible for regulating the selling activities of insurance companies, the authorisation and prudential supervision of these companies is the responsibility of the DTI, a non-FSA authority. The fund management activities of insurance companies are regulated by IMRO.

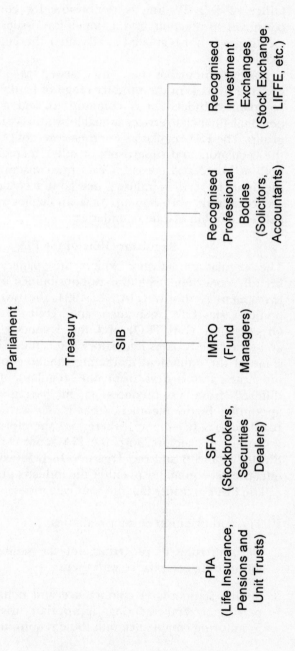

**Figure 1:
The Regulatory Bodies**

Parliament

Treasury

SIB

PIA
(Life Insurance,
Pensions and
Unit Trusts)

SFA
(Stockbrokers,
Securities
Dealers)

IMRO
(Fund
Managers)

Recognised
Professional
Bodies
(Solicitors,
Accountants)

Recognised
Investment
Exchanges
(Stock Exchange,
LIFFE, etc.)

While the PIA is responsible for personal pensions, the DSS is responsible for the regulation of occupational pensions. The Office of Fair Trading is responsible for consumer credit, consumer protection and competition issues. The sale of mortgages is not regulated at all under the Financial Services Act.

Further anomalies have now arisen as a result of the growing overlap in the product range of banks and insurance companies. Indeed, it is common to find a full range of personal financial services available within a single corporate group. The FSA regulators are therefore obliged to liaise with the regulators and supervisors of other financial institutions, both at home and abroad. Given the constant innovation in the financial services industry, new contracts and new activities are constantly throwing up new anomalies created by the existence of out-of-date boundaries.

Regulatory Rôle of the PIA

The regulatory activities which this paper addresses are broadly congruent with the responsibilities of the Personal Investment Authority (PIA). In 1994, the two self-regulating bodies, the Life Assurance and Unit Trust Regulatory Organisation (LAUTRO) and the Financial Intermediaries and Mortgage Brokers Regulatory Association (FIMBRA) (plus some of the equivalent marketing functions of IMRO), were integrated into a new 'front line' regulator, the PIA, which differed from its predecessors in having a majority of appointed Board members (that is, it was no longer self-regulating). In theory, there is therefore a three-tier institutional structure, with the PIA reporting to Parliament through the SIB and the Treasury. In practice, the PIA lacks effective accountability to either the industry or to Parliament.

The PIA's activities fall into four categories:

1. The authorisation of intermediaries.

2. Devising rules of procedure for the selling process, and monitoring compliance with them.

3. Setting standards of competence and behaviour for sales personnel, and defining appropriate training schemes; monitoring compliance with these requirements.

4. Defining and monitoring procedures for the consideration and resolution of consumer complaints.

While there may be criticism of the way in which the PIA goes about its tasks under headings 1, 3 and 4, there is little dispute that these are appropriate measures to ensure fair trading – that is, to maintain a market in which buyers and sellers can take part with confidence. In most other countries, similar functions are performed by the regulatory authorities.

It is the activities of the PIA under heading 2 which are the most costly and the most controversial. Is it justifiable for a regulatory authority to prescribe rules of procedure for sellers of personal investment services, to require documentation of these procedures, and to monitor compliance with them? These are not practices which are generally followed in other countries.

Regulation in Other Countries

Other countries have tried to resolve the problem of quality uncertainty for the consumer by imposing quality controls on the process of supply. Three things in principle may be subject to control:

1. The suppliers.

2. The products.

3. The selling agents.

The first of these is almost universally practised: most countries exclude from their markets those companies judged by the regulatory authorities to be deficient in one of a number of qualities affecting their capacity to satisfy the consumer.

The second is practised in some countries, although not in the UK. The Third Life Directive has obliged many continental European states which had hitherto strictly regulated their companies and their products to relax these controls. In response, rules are now being tightened for the regulation of selling agents. The Third Life Directive lays down extensive requirements regarding the information to be provided to the policyholder before a contract is concluded.

[33]

Significantly, however, the scope of an EU Recommendation[4] laying down the principles which member-states should follow in stipulating standards for intermediaries, says nothing about the regulation of selling procedures, nor even about codes of conduct. It confines itself to standards of professional competence and to the compulsory registration of persons acting as intermediaries. It also encourages member-states to lay down sanctions to enforce these measures.

The German insurance industry has for long had a register of intermediaries, run by a self-regulating professional body. In response to the relaxation of German regulations on companies and products, the industry has recently set up a professional training and examination programme, which is also self-regulated. The German government has therefore felt it unnecessary to take any further legislative steps to implement the EU recommendation. German industry, however, is now calling for its self-regulatory practices to be given the force of law.[5] They want neither 'comprehensive and detailed regulations for authorisation of insurance intermediaries nor statutory codes of conduct'.[6]

In the United States, responsibility for the regulation of most life assurance activities lies with the individual States. Few, if any, have statutory codes of conduct concerning the behaviour of their selling agents, although some, as in Europe, register and authorise these agents to practice, and attempt to control their competence. The States, however, do not monitor the selling activities of insurance companies on a continuing basis. They investigate in response to consumer complaints and press inquiries.

Problems of market misconduct have been reported in the United States at much the same time as in the UK. For

<hr>

4   *EC Recommendation on Insurance Intermediaries* (XV/104/91), adopted 18 December 1991. The European Commission's Directorate for Financial Services (DGXV) has followed this up with a Green Paper, *Financial Services: Meeting Consumers' Expectations,* issued in May 1996.

5   They claim that this is because of considerations of consumer protection: they assert that intensified competition will mean that self-regulation will become ineffective. The real reason is probably the same as obtains in Ireland: the fear that foreign competitors will not abide by the rules of self-regulation.

6   E. Jannott, 'Effects of the De-regulation of Supervision on the Selling of Insurance', *Geneva Papers,* No. 74, January 1995, p.7.

example, the US Prudential is facing a series of lawsuits over 'churning',[7] while Metropolitan Life was fined $1·5 million in 1994 by the State of Pennsylvania, also for churning. The industry has become alarmed by the damage which market misconduct has done to its reputation, and the American Council of Life Insurance is drafting a voluntary code of standards.

At the same time there is a movement towards the relaxation of statutory regulation. New York State's new Superintendent of Insurance, as part of a review of the regulations mandated by the Governor, has written to insurers licensed in the State, asking for their help in analysing the economic burden imposed by regulations, including the cost of complying with their provisions and their impact on jobs and competition. In a recent NY Insurance Department bulletin, he wrote that his goal is to create a competitive atmosphere in the State. 'I believe by stimulating competition, we can create opportunities for new products, for certain growth, and ultimately, for prices that will find their lowest mark because of competitive forces.'[8]

---

[7] The name given in the trade to the practice of switching a customer's investments unnecessarily, so that commission may be earned on the transaction.

[8] *Best's Review*, Vol. 96, No. 2, June 1995; N. D. Boynton, *Market Conduct: A Global Tidal Wave*, New York: LIMRA, 1995.

IV. THE FAILURE OF THE FINANCIAL SERVICES ACT

Since legislators and regulators take it for granted that they act in the best interests of consumers, it is fitting to ask what consumers think of the effectiveness of the regulatory framework established by the Financial Services Act. The verdict of the Consumers' Association is categorical:

'The Financial Services Act was supposed to protect investors. But now, ten years on, it's clear that the Act has failed.' [1]

When Professor Gower, the architect of the Act, was asked in 1991 how he thought it had been implemented, he is reported to have replied: 'It's a total disaster.' [2]

What is the basis for these reactions? A considerable amount of evidence has accumulated since 1986 that the present system of regulation is not working, in the sense that it is not serving the interests of consumers. This is despite several changes in personnel which have occurred since that date.

Fraud

The DTI's invitation to Professor Gower in 1981 to review the existing statutory framework of investor protection appears to have been prompted by a failure to secure convictions under the Prevention of Fraud (Investments) Act 1958, and by the political reaction aroused by a number of minor but well-publicised failures of financial firms involving suspicion of fraud (Norton Warburg, Doxford – see Section III, above, p.28). When the Financial Services Act came into force seven years later, the principal concern of the authorities still appears to have been to reduce the likelihood of fraud.

Subsequent events, such as the Barlow Clowes,[3] Maxwell, Levitt and other less well-publicised cases suggest that the new

---

[1]   *Which?* magazine, June 1996, p.40.

[2]   Quoted in *Money Marketing*, 2 November 1995, p.30.

[3]   Although the offences committed at Barlow Clowes took place before the Financial Services Act came into operation, the subsequent inquiry carried out

regulatory framework has been unable to do this. According to the Annual Reports of the Serious Fraud Office (SFO), the number of cases of fraud on investors under investigation by the SFO shows no downward trend.

In the Barlow Clowes case, private investors lost £191 million which they thought had been invested in government bonds, but some of which had in fact been used by Mr Peter Clowes to finance his personal expenditures. In the years up to 1991 IMRO failed to stop the disappearance of nearly £440 million in pension assets from a fund management company controlled by the late Robert Maxwell.

Roger Levitt allegedly defrauded several life assurance companies of some £59 million. He originally faced 62 charges of theft, fraud and deception but, after plea bargaining, he was sentenced to 180 hours of community service upon conviction on a small number of lesser charges. George Walker was acquitted of masterminding a £19 million fraud at Brent Walker.

By its nature, fraud is impossible to eradicate. But its incidence could be expected to be reduced if the deterrent effects are sufficiently strong. Deterrence requires a high probability of conviction combined with severity of sentence. But so low have been the rates of conviction, and so derisory the punishments, that it would not be surprising to find the London financial markets becoming an increasing target for frauds in the future.

Market Misconduct

More recently, the attention of politicians and regulators has switched from the prevention of fraud to the control of market misconduct. Market misconduct, variously known as mal-practice or mis-selling, occurs in that grey area between fraud and incompetence which in other industries might be described as unfair trading. In the personal investment market, the principal concern is that many people may be sold contracts inappropriate to their needs – that is, they are given bad advice by the selling agent.

The simplest and most widely accepted measure of the extent to which bad advice is prevalent in any personal investment market is the rate at which policies are sur-

---

by the DTI showed that the same events could still have occurred under the present regulatory framework.

rendered before they mature. This is a measure used by the regulators themselves. Like all such measures, the 'lapse rate' has its limitations. As a long-term investment policy reaches the middle of its life, changes in circumstances and poor investment returns may play a part in a decision by a saver to surrender his policy or make it paid-up, but the most common reason for lapses in the first few years of a policy is bad advice. We therefore take early lapses, to be precise, the ratio of forfeitures to new business, to be an appropriate measure of changes in the extent of mis-selling over time.[4]

When one examines forfeiture rates from 1985 to 1994, the statistics show that while things have improved slightly of late, the experience in 1994 is still little better than that of 10 years earlier.[5] In other words, after 10 years of the Financial Services Act, the degree of mis-selling seems not to have improved (Figure 2). The apparent improvement after 1991 may be due to more effective competition (see Section VII, below, p.66).

Not only has there been little change in these lapse rates, but the levels of some particular rates give cause for concern. For example, 15 per cent of all personal pensions sold by company representatives (salesmen) are being lapsed in the first year. If one takes lapse rates across the whole market, together with the number of regular premium policies sold, the result on first year lapses alone represents an annual loss of around £150-200 million.[6]

In principle, in order to know whether an unsuitable contract has been sold to a particular individual, one would have to wait until the completion of the contract to make a categorical judgement.

There have, however, been clusters of cases recently where the discrepancy between expected outcomes (and sometimes actual outcomes) and the needs and circumstances of the buyers

---

[4] Forfeitures represent those terminations that do not give rise to a payment and therefore mainly include early lapses.

[5] *Persistency*, London: Mercantile & General Reinsurance Company and Jardine Arber and Company, 1995, p.23.

[6] Jean Eaglesham, 'Has The System Protected The Retail Consumer?', paper delivered to a Conference on The Finance Services Act After Ten Years, organised by the Centre for the Study of Financial Innovation, London, March 1996.

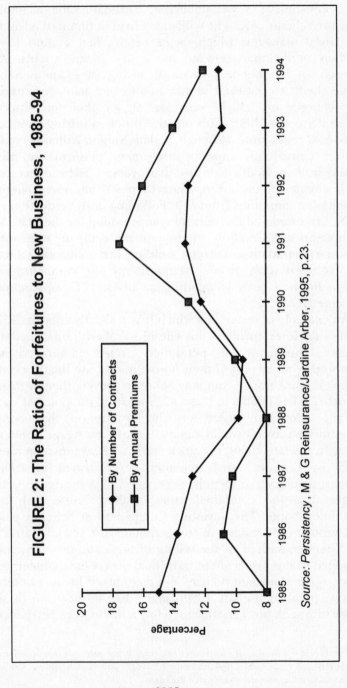

FIGURE 2: The Ratio of Forfeitures to New Business, 1985-94

Source: Persistency, M & G Reinsurance/Jardine Arber, 1995, p.23.

have constituted a well-publicised 'scandal'. One example concerns clients of Knight Williams, a firm of financial advisers and fund managers which, at its height, had around £500 million under management and some 25,000 clients. Although an independent financial adviser, it recommended some clients to put their money into its own managed funds, the charges on which were far higher than on similar investments elsewhere. This practice is not an infringement of any FSA regulation, although, unless Knight Williams could deliver consistently superior investment performance, this would lead inevitably to worse-than-average performance for their clients. In the event, more than 400 aggrieved clients sought compensation from SIB. Following an investigation in 1994, SIB estimated the value of compensation for the first 152 complaints at £3 million, whereupon the company went into voluntary liquidation, thereby avoiding the obligation to pay any compensation at all. Responsibility for compensation claims has now been assumed by the Investors Compensation Scheme (ICS).

An example of mis-selling which began shortly after the FSA came into force involved the sale of so-called 'home income plans'. Thousands of pensioners were encouraged to remortgage all or part of their houses and to use the proceeds to invest in insurance company bonds to provide them with an income. The viability of these schemes from the point of view of the consumer rested on the assumption that bond investment returns would always outstrip mortgage interest rates. In the late 1980s, the stock market fell and interest rates rose. By the time such schemes were banned in 1990, thousands of elderly people were left with a mortgage debt larger than the combined value of their house and the insurance bond. The Investors Compensation Scheme paid out a total of £50 million in compensation to 2,500 investors.[7]

Other accusations of the selling of life assurance contracts unsuited to the needs of the individual buyers have concerned mortgage endowment policies and guaranteed income bonds. At one point in the late 1980s, more than 80 per cent of all those who took out a mortgage to buy a house were persuaded

---

[7] The ICS is required to try to recover the sums it has paid out from parties it believes are responsible, and currently has legal actions outstanding against several building societies which sold the plans.

by the lenders to take out low-cost mortgage endowments as a means of repaying those mortgages. There can be little doubt that this high proportion reflected in part the commission which the lenders received for selling these policies. Likewise, a variety of guaranteed high income bonds is being sold at the present time. A typical example is one which offers a guaranteed income of 10 per cent per annum with full return of capital after five years, provided that the FT-SE 100 Index and the S&P 500 Index are higher after five years than they were at the time of purchase.

Both these types of contracts illustrate the great difficulty of deciding whether bad advice has been given to a purchaser. If future prospects are judged with reference to the recent past, then both types of contract would seem to represent good advice *at the time it was given* (leaving aside the question of the suitability of these contracts to the financial circumstances of particular individuals). In the late 1980s, house prices had been rising for almost a decade, and stock market returns in the recent past had exceeded mortgage interest rates. Today, the possibility of a fall over five years in the FT-SE and S&P Indices is almost zero, if we are to judge by the experience of the past 20 years. If, however, we look back 60 years or more, then there is a probability of around 20 per cent that purchasers of such plans might lose half their capital.

It is clear that the quality of any advice must be judged in the light of knowledge prevailing at the time, and not with hindsight, although questions may be asked about whether the risks are understood by the buyer or even known by the seller. What is also clear is that, except in extreme circumstances, judgements about the quality of advice can only be based on subjective evaluation, not objective measurement. Yet the regulatory bodies set up under the FSA have sought to prescribe 'best advice' as if it was something that could be measured objectively. In attempting to do so, they have imposed significant burdens of cost on the selling process, costs which have directly or indirectly been borne by the consumer.

The most celebrated recent allegations of market misconduct concern the selling of personal pensions. As this episode has received so much publicity and is still unresolved it merits more extended consideration.

Mis-Selling of Personal Pensions

About eight million personal pensions were sold in the UK between 1988 and 1995. Some were sold to people who were in occupational pension schemes and who were advised to transfer out of these schemes and to take out personal pensions in their place. To what extent was this bad advice? For those who were in well-funded schemes where the prospective pension was protected against inflation by state guarantee, as was the case in most public sector schemes, it would be very difficult to argue that it was good advice to leave these schemes in favour of a personal pension where there is no employer contribution. But even in these extreme cases, circumstances can be constructed where it could be argued that bad advice was not necessarily given.

For the huge majority of pension transfer cases, whether bad advice was given (and therefore payment of compensation can be justified) depends on what the advisers said, almost impossible to recollect many years later, and what the buyer perceived his needs to be at the time, also subject to change with the passage of time.

The true scale of the problem is still unknown. Some 560,000 'urgent' cases have been identified by the PIA for priority review. By the end of September 1996, 14,000 people had been offered compensation totalling £26·75 million.[8]

In the case of pensions mis-selling, the regulatory failure has been three-fold. *First,* the regulatory authorities ignored warnings given as early as the late 1980s by leading figures in the industry and by reports in the press. [9]

Second, when SIB finally reacted in 1993, they commissioned a report which greatly exaggerated the scale of the problem by suggesting that up to 1·5 million people had been wrongly advised to start a personal pension, and that compensation would eventually amount to some £4 billion. This report raised unwarranted expectations of compensation on the part of many buyers of personal pensions, while at the same time inflicting a severe blow to public confidence in the industry (see below).

---

[8] 'Secret PIA document names biggest pensions offenders', *The Independent,* 30 October 1996, p.18.

[9] Eaglesham, *op.cit.*

Third, SIB published a timetable and procedure for reviewing and compensating cases of pensions mis-selling. It has repeatedly failed to meet all its deadlines, including those for providing guidelines for compensation.

Chastened by this experience, SIB has abandoned the idea of implementing a similar review of 'rebate-only' pensions, and instead is calling for voluntary action on the part of the companies concerned. This problem concerns those people who were advised to opt out of the state earnings related pension scheme (SERPS) and into a personal pension, and who subsequently contracted back in again. In these cases, flat-rate charges made by companies administering the policies erode the value of smaller funds.

More than five million people have opted out of SERPS in the past eight years, but research commissioned by SIB indicated that only 4 per cent of these may have been disadvantaged, with average losses of £78 per annum.

Loss of Confidence in the Market

Partly as a result of the publicity given to the earlier cases of mis-selling, the volume of sales of personal pensions fell sharply in 1994 and 1995. In the latter year 1·1 million personal pensions were taken out compared with 1·8 million in 1993. New sales of personal pensions had been falling for five years.

While primary responsibility for mis-selling must rest with the individual sales agents concerned and their employers, the actions of the regulators have aggravated the situation. As we have seen, they allowed the scale of the problem to be greatly exaggerated. Furthermore, by imposing highly publicised fines on a number of well-known companies, the impression was given to consumers that all companies in the industry are equally guilty, that none can be trusted. Few consumers were aware that these sanctions were in most cases imposed for failure to comply with the prescribed procedure rather than for actual misconduct. In addition, SIB took three years to conclude compensation arrangements. As a result, the press was able to damage severely the reputation of the industry, and to destroy consumers' confidence in the market by painting all of its members in the blackest of colours.[10]

---

[10] Bernard Levin, *The Times*, 2 August 1994.

The proportion of households which protect themselves through purchasing life insurance has fallen by nearly 10 percentage points over the last 10 years. The regulatory system may have contributed to this decline in the volume of sales in two other ways. Regulatory requirements have extended substantially the time taken to sell even the most basic investment contracts. Under the Financial Services Act, any firm or individual which sells investment contracts must have a detailed knowledge of its potential customers' financial circumstances and deliver the best advice based on that knowledge. In order to prove to the regulators that best advice has been given, companies have felt obliged to come up with 'fact-finds' – that is, questionnaires which can run to more than 20 pages and can take up to three or even four hours to complete.[11] Customers are not usually prepared to devote so much time to an exercise which they often regard as intrusive and time-wasting, especially where small sums may be involved. Many potential buyers have therefore been put off by these regulatory requirements.

At the same time, many sales forces have been withdrawn because of the increased costs which this type of regulation has imposed on their operation. Increased costs have also contributed to a reduction in the number of independent financial advisers.

In these ways, consumers have been discouraged from buying contracts which they would otherwise have bought, and which it would have been in their interests to buy. Thus, the consumer is disadvantaged in the same way as if he had been sold an unsuitable contract.

A further distortion has arisen from regulatory attempts to control the flow of information between buyer and seller. These attempts have led regulators to establish an untenable distinction between 'information', 'advice' and 'execution-only' business. The volume of the last type of business is growing not because there is a great demand for it (on the

---

[11] 'The sales process has changed over the past five years – where once selling the appropriate insurance with a mortgage would have taken 45 minutes to an hour, now it takes a minimum of three hours and in some cases two meetings with the customer. The vast majority of customers don't want that when buying a house.' (Stephen Shipperley, Chief Executive of Connor Residential, quoted in the *Financial Times*, 15 August 1995.)

contrary, most people are in real need of proper financial planning advice), but because many people find it preferable to having to provide a large amount of information and to receiving in return an equally large amount of unwanted information from the seller.

Ironically, this loss of confidence in the market has been brought about at a time when the Government wishes to encourage people to move away from reliance on state pension provision and into the private pensions market.

Anti-Competitive Behaviour

In his Wincott Memorial Lecture, delivered in November 1995, Sir Bryan Carsberg said:

> 'When I was regulator of the telecommunications industry, I learned, when facing a regulatory problem, always to ask whether progress could be made by promoting competition more effectively, before turning to the possible need for more detailed regulation.'[12]

This is not a thought that appears to have occurred either to Professor Gower, the architect of the Financial Services Act, or to any of those subsequently charged with its implementation. From 1986 onwards, the SIB, urged on by the industry, fought a rearguard action against the OFT's recommendation requiring companies and agents to disclose to consumers information on the prices and commission payments they received on policies sold.[13] Disclosure came into force on 1 January 1995; thus the SIB was able to hold up the development of price competition in the industry for almost nine years. Today, the same organisation unblushingly identifies disclosure as one of the principal measures for investor protection.[14]

---

[12] Sir Bryan Carsberg, *Competition Regulation The British Way: Jaguar or Dinosaur?*, Occasional Paper 97, London: Institute of Economic Affairs, 1996, p.10.

[13] 'The risks of adopting disclosure requirements that conveyed an apparent, but spurious sense of accuracy, a misleading sense of authority, and an unjustified sense of relevance seemed to the Board to outweigh any potential benefits.' (*Life Assurance Companies – Disclosure of Expenses and Charges*, London: SIB, 1986.)

[14] *The Background To Investor Protection*, London: SIB, 1996.

Costs of Regulation

Regulatory procedures have led to the imposition of a burden of costs, disproportionate in relation to benefits, borne initially by companies and their agents but ultimately passed on to the consumers,[15] those whom the regulations aim to protect. Estimates of the size of some of these costs are discussed in Section VI (below, pp.55-57).

Amongst the costs which cannot be quantified but which are nevertheless important are those which are incurred by the inhibition of innovation. Prior to the Financial Services Act, the UK life assurance industry was recognised to be among the most innovative in the world. However, some of the regulatory bodies set up under that Act have not been prepared to review and sanction new products prior to their launch, but have reserved the right to carry out retrospective reviews some years later. A notable example was the introduction of single premium with-profits bonds in 1990. These products were on the market for some two years before the regulators indicated they had some concerns about them. By that time, several billion pounds' worth had been sold.

More recently, the Government itself created a new class of product by permitting some flexibility in connection with the purchase of annuities out of retirement pension funds. It is entirely possible that, in some years' time, yet another retrospective review will be undertaken in which companies will be criticised for their selling approach to this class of product, again undermining consumer confidence in the market.

If regulators are prepared to decide that they have concerns with a product only some years after its launch, then the potential exposure of the supplying companies becomes very large, with an inevitably adverse impact on the rate of product innovation.

---

15 Many people may find it difficult to believe that regulatory costs incurred by firms in a competitive industry will necessarily be passed on to the customer. It is true that, *in the short term*, some of the burden of costs could fall on shareholders' capital, and on the incomes of managers and of intermediaries. However, *in the long term*, if managers, shareholders and intermediaries did not earn the rates of return they anticipated before the regulatory costs were incurred, their services would be withdrawn, and the whole burden of the cost would therefore have to be passed on to the customer.

V. REASONS FOR REGULATORY FAILURE

In Section IV we showed some evidence of the failure of the regulatory framework established by the 1986 Financial Services Act. Why has this happened? In this section, we discuss three main reasons.

- *First,* there has been some confusion about the objectives of regulation in the minds of the regulators.

- *Second,* priority has been given to the wrong method of regulation, namely the prescription of detailed rules of procedure which buyers and sellers are obliged to follow.

- *Third,* the organisation of the regulatory institutions is such that they lack accountability, with a resulting proliferation of all the problems of bureaucracy.

Taken together, these features of the present regulatory system mean that it is fundamentally flawed. Blame is not to be attached to the individuals working within the system, but to the system itself. Only by understanding what is wrong with it will it be possible to construct a better system in the future.

Confused Objectives

The implementation of the Financial Services Act has been characterised hitherto by an absence of clear thinking[1] on the part of the regulatory authorities about their objectives and methods.[2] They saw it as their priority to create rule books:

---

[1] A sure sign of a reluctance to think clearly is the practice of resorting to metaphor when plain English will do. Speaking about the current regulatory framework to a conference of the Society of Financial Advisers, the Economic Secretary to the Treasury, Angela Knight MP, said: 'I know there are rough edges, but it is much better to pull together to sort things out than to throw the baby out with the bathwater and start again.' (Quoted in *The Times,* 2 December 1995.)

[2] The OFT has produced a stream of useful analytical papers on the marketing of financial services over the past 10 years, but this body lies outside the scope of the Financial Services Act.

'SIB's first major task was to construct a rule book which ... ensured that the objective of investor protection envisaged in the Act was translated into practical terms regarding the conduct of investment business. The rules are designed to outlaw malpractice, to raise standards, and to require proper financial and other management disciplines within investment firms.' [3]

The issues of whether the rules would be likely to diminish malpractice or whether it was appropriate for a regulator to attempt to raise standards or to act as a management consultant to the industry were simply not addressed. Nor was the concept of 'investor protection' questioned.

The concept of 'investor protection' as the central objective of the regulatory régime is flawed for at least two reasons:

- *First*, it raises in the minds of consumers the unattainable expectation of complete protection whenever they make a decision to invest. This has set in motion a vicious circle, whereby frustrated consumer expectations lead to increasingly prescriptive regulation, followed in turn by rising costs and further disappointment.

- *Second*, it implies that *all* sellers are untrustworthy, and that the regulators know better than the sellers how to satisfy the buyers' needs.

No reputable company in any industry would accept the proposition that its customers need protection from the company. The implications to the contrary implicit in the phrase 'investor protection', exacerbated by the prescriptive method of regulation, undermine consumer confidence in the entire industry. In the case of a mutual insurance company, the notion that its policyholders need protection from themselves is slightly absurd.[4]

There is the further implication that investor protection must operate against market forces, rather than with them. Gower wrote that 'there is a tension between market efficiency

---

[3] *The Background to Investor Protection*, London: SIB, 1996, p.6.

[4] Although management might redistribute income between groups of policyholders, those who feel thus harmed can protect themselves by exercising their powers of ownership. In evidence to the Treasury Committee, SIB Chairman Andrew Large admitted that it was 'bizarre' to penalise policyholders twice by imposing fines on mutual companies.

and investor protection which often pull in different directions', and that a free and efficient market would 'not afford protection to investors which anyone today would regard as adequate'.[5] These statements show that Gower[6] did not understand the meaning of the term 'market efficiency': if markets were truly 'efficient' in the sense of neo-classical economic theory, there would be no need for 'investor protection' (see Section II above, pp.16).

Since the benefits to consumers of even an inadequately working market are incomparably greater than the benefits which regulators can provide, it makes sense for regulators to work with market forces rather than against them. In the personal investment market, as in any other, it is to competition that consumers must look primarily for their needs and interests to be protected, and only secondarily to official regulation. Recently, there have been some encouraging signs on the part of regulators of a willingness to reconsider the fundamental issues of the objectives and methods of regulation.[7]

Legislators and policy-makers who have the interests of consumers at heart should also be directing their efforts to making the market more competitive, and new regulation should be designed with the primacy of this objective in mind. New principles of regulation are proposed in Section VIII (below, pp.68-77).

Prescriptive Procedures

It may be said that this is all very well in theory, but in practice competition is not going to prevent the notorious commission-hungry salesman from pressing unwanted and expensive contracts on the uninformed buyer. The answer of the regulators to this problem has been to prepare books of rules

---

[5] Cmnd.9125, *op.cit.*, para. 1.16.

[6] Gower's disdain for analysis was shown when he wrote that 'in assessing the optimum degree of regulation I have not attempted any sort of cost-benefit analysis, partly because I am not competent to undertake it, and partly because I am sceptical about its practicability'. (*Review of Investor Protection*, Report, Part I, Cmnd.9125, January 1984, para. 1.16.) Ironically, SIB set up in 1995 a unit to perform cost-benefit analysis. The double irony is that Gower was right to be sceptical about the likely effectiveness of cost-benefit analysis in this context. The reasons for this are discussed in Section VI.

[7] See PIA, *Regulatory Plan: Second Year*, London: PIA, July 1996.

specifying procedures to be followed by sellers. But the attempt to control quality of advice by obliging the sellers and their agents to follow certain prescribed procedures is unlikely to succeed for several reasons.

Those who wilfully give bad advice will be undeterred by having to follow procedures; rogues will cheerfully tick boxes, honest men may get confused. Indeed, the more complex the rules, the greater the opportunity for concealing dishonesty.

Nor will this prevent mis-selling through commission bias. Since judgements about the quality of advice (such as the suitability of a product to a consumer's particular needs) are likely to be subjective in the great majority of cases, they cannot be judged by objective criteria. The lack of progress of the current pensions review being organised by the PIA amply demonstrates the futility of attempting to impose objective criteria on what are fundamentally subjective issues.

Furthermore, lengthy procedures themselves constitute a form of mis-selling, by deterring some consumers from taking out contracts which it would be in their interests to do. Following prescribed procedures is also very costly. The direct costs of selling a personal investment contract have at least doubled under the present rules.

A less obvious but nonetheless real cost of prescriptive regulation is the inhibition of innovation. The insistence on sticking to prescribed procedures inhibits the development of new business processes, whether these be the adoption of electronic selling methods or the provision of advice through expert systems. (See also Section IV above, 'Costs of Regulation', p.46.)

It is significant that, with the possible exception of Australia, no other country prescribes procedures to be followed by selling agents in their personal investment market. Many countries do have prescribed procedures to be followed by manufacturers in the case of health and safety or of environmental protection legislation, and by government departments in the case of the prevention of fraud. Such prescriptive rules have proved to be very costly in relation to their effectiveness. For example, the Department of Defense in the United States allegedly spends more on procedures to prevent fraudulent travel claims from members of the armed forces than it spends on actual travel.[8]

---

8 Philip Howard, *The Death of Commonsense*, New York: Random House, 1994.

Recently, the PIA has begun to entertain proposals from companies for abbreviated fact-finds. But improvements on this front have been offset by an onerous new battery of record-keeping requirements introduced under its new Training and Competence initiative.

Lack of Accountability

While the lower regulatory bodies are nominally accountable for their behaviour to Parliament through the Chancellor of the Exchequer, in practice they are effectively insulated from any such accountability.

First, the attenuation of control characteristic of bureaucracies, in which much of what is done by lower ranking officials is unknown to those of higher rank, is exacerbated by two features of the present regulatory system. There are effectively six stages to the process of getting a major decision finalised, as each of the three regulatory tiers (see Figure 1) has both an executive and non-executive hierarchy. This not only dilutes responsibility, but adds unnecessary cost and delay.

Second, as a relic of its self-regulatory origins, the PIA enjoys some freedom to act independently of its nominally superior body, the SIB, a freedom which it exploits to the full. The result is a dangerous deficit of accountability, whose consequences may only become fully apparent in a crisis. In such circumstances, SIB and PIA are likely to dispute amongst themselves as to which is responsible for what, while blaming others for any delay. As we have seen, SIB took three years to conclude its guidelines for the compensation criteria for cases of mis-selling pensions. The theory of public choice (see Section II, above, p.25-26) asserts that employees in the public sector are no different from those in the private sector in their motivations. Self-interest as well as altruism is found in both sectors. Only the constraints are different. In the private sector there is the discipline of the market; in the public sector there should be accountability. Where this is lacking, it is not surprising to find examples of empire building and struggles for power both between and within regulatory authorities.[9]

---

[9] See, for example, 'SIB Undermines Other Regulators', *The Independent*, 28 June 1995.

Empire Building

The regulators continuously desire to expand the scope of their activities. Currently, for example, the PIA is seeking to extend its regulatory powers from the investment market to the market for protection products and mortgages.

No Incentive for Controlling Costs

SIB simply passes on its annual increments in cost to the tiers below it which in turn add their own costs and pass them on ultimately to the industry in the form of increased fees for 'membership'. The City Research Project has estimated that the direct administrative costs (excluding compliance and other costs) of all regulatory bodies in the whole of the financial services sector was 80 per cent higher in real terms in 1992 than it had been in 1987, before the Financial Services Act came into force.[10] Peacock and Bannock estimate that between 1988 and 1994 the basic regulatory fees of a typical financial adviser increased by 74 per cent in real terms, while those fees plus mandatory contributions to the Investors Compensation Scheme plus professional indemnity insurance (but excluding compliance costs) were estimated to have risen by 577 per cent in real terms.[11]

Arbitrary Behaviour

The existing regulations permit regulators a degree of arbitrariness which is not conducive to the confidence of participants in the market. Originally, the PIA refused to approve a company's selling procedures as being 'compliant', reserving the right always to make *ex post* judgements. It never signs off any business it has audited as being satisfactory. Companies wishing to minimise the risk of penalties are therefore obliged to err in the direction of time-consuming, costly and customer-unfriendly 'fact-finds'. Confronted with the innovation of investment contracts being offered for sale by telephone without advice (to avoid the existing regulations), the PIA is faced with the inevitably arbitrary

---

[10] J. Franks and S. Schaefer, 'The Costs and Effectiveness of the UK Financial Regulatory System', The City Research Project, London Business School, March 1993.

[11] A. T. Peacock and G. Bannock, *The Rationale of Financial Services Regulation*, London: Graham Bannock & Partners Limited, June 1995.

choice of either banning such transactions (thereby depriving consumers of identifiable benefits), or abandoning the rules which currently impose heavy costs on sellers distributing through the traditional channels.

Dissipation of Resources in Power Struggles

Recent evidence to the Treasury Select Committee confirms publicly the existence of extensive struggles for power and influence within and between the regulatory bodies.[12]

Anomalies of Regulation

The boundaries between different regulatory régimes are not always congruent with boundaries between different classes of financial service. This gives rise to anomalies in the treatment of services which are competing with each other in the eyes of the consumer, but which fall under different regulatory régimes.

The regulatory system currently treats most life insurance and pension policies in the same way, but differently from all other financial services. The reality is that some life insurance products compete with unit trusts. Likewise, some bank deposits are close substitutes for some life insurance products. When there is a heavy regulatory régime for life insurance and pensions, a less onerous régime for unit trusts, an even lighter régime for banking services, and no régime at all for such investments as ostriches, then distortions will inevitably arise, leading to a switch of business away from the more regulated to the less regulated products. A similar situation arises with income protection and critical illness policies: some critical illness and some income protection policies fall outside the scope of the Act while others fall within it.

A further anomaly arises when some elements of a financial package of services operate under a different regulatory régime from others. When buying a house, a consumer may take out a mortgage together with a life assurance policy and an investment contract to repay the loan. While the endow-

---

[12] 'It is clear that in-fighting among the regulators and the jostling for position in any potential new structure is not helping to enhance the public perception of the regulatory system nor adding anything to the achievement of investor protection.' (House of Commons, Session 1994/95, Treasury and Civil Service Committee, Sixth Report: *The Regulation of Financial Services in the United Kingdom*, House of Commons Paper 332, Vol. I, October 1995.)

ment policy is very heavily regulated, the mortgage is hardly regulated at all, even though mortgages are one of the largest financial commitments which a typical consumer makes.

Yet another type of anomaly occurs when companies being investigated for an alleged malpractice are treated more severely than their competitors being investigated for a similar offence by a different regulatory body. An example of this arose when two companies investigated by IMRO for allegedly giving bad advice over pensions transfers discovered they would have been disciplined more leniently had they been regulated by the PIA.[13] These anomalies suggest the need for a single-tier regulatory authority whose scope should encompass a broad range of personal financial services.

Company Pension Schemes

Company pension schemes fall into one of two categories: either they are defined contribution (DC) schemes or they are defined benefit (DB) schemes. As its name implies, the contribution level of a DC scheme is fixed in advance. The size of the member's pension depends on how well his or her individual investment fund performs. The employer does not have to pay higher contributions if the performance is poor, as is the case with the DB scheme in which members' pensions are set as a proportion of their final salary. While, at the present time, the assets of DC schemes are small compared to those held by DB schemes, new rules on solvency imposed by the 1995 Pensions Act impose significant compliance burdens on employers with DB schemes which will not have to be met by employers with DC schemes.

Thus, the recent Pensions Act legislation, intended to benefit the employee, is likely to have the opposite effect. It will diminish the attractiveness of DB schemes in the eyes of employers, schemes which on the whole offer employees greater benefits than do DC schemes.

---

[13] *Financial Times*, 12 January 1995.

VI. THE COSTS AND BENEFITS OF REGULATION

The costs of regulation can be divided into three categories:

1. *Costs of administration:* These comprise the costs of operating the regulatory system – that is, the salaries and other costs of the regulatory agencies – together with the relevant costs of those units of government departments concerned with the regulation of retail financial services.

2. *Compliance costs:* These are the costs, borne in the first instance by the industry, incurred in complying with the regulations. As we shall see, these costs may be between five and 10 times greater than the direct costs of administration. What appears to distinguish the UK system of regulation of retail investment is the large indirect burden of compliance costs which it places on consumers through the industry.

3. *Excess burden:* These are the costs which result from the distortions to the market resulting from regulation. Examples include sales not concluded because consumers are alienated by paperwork, and losses to consumers from impediments to the development of new products and new channels of distribution. Raising the costs of operation of all providers makes it too costly to administer marginal business. Low-income, small-premium savers are squeezed out of the market and denied the benefits of investment management services. Although difficult to quantify, these costs may be very large and are borne by society as a whole.

Estimates of Costs

1. Costs of Administration

Although a small part of the costs of administering the regulatory system is borne by taxpayers, most costs are paid for by the industry, through obligatory membership fees to the appropriate regulatory bodies. Costs which fall into this category are therefore readily ascertainable.

2. Costs of Compliance

While it is easy to define compliance costs as those which are wholly and necessarily incurred by providers and intermediaries for the purposes of complying with regulation, and which would not have been incurred in the absence of regulation, it is less easy in practice to identify such costs unambiguously. While it is clear that the salaries of members of a firm's compliance department fall into this category, the attribution of other costs is more open to doubt. For example, how far should the costs of improved selling procedures be attributed to regulation, and how much to improved marketing techniques? These are questions which do not admit of any objective answers, and therefore no precise estimates of this category of costs are possible. It is, however, possible to attempt an assessment of their order of magnitude.

The first such estimate was provided by Lomax,[1] who estimated that for all those financial services which fell under the auspices of the Financial Services Act, costs of compliance would be about four times the costs of administration – that is, 80 per cent of total regulatory costs.

Later the City Research Project (CRP),[2] using 1992 data, analysed compliance costs in some depth for a number of sectors of financial services, excluding, however, life assurance and personal financial advice. For securities firms, they found that compliance costs were between 1·9 and 2·5 times direct costs, and for investment management firms, about 1·8 times.

The first systematic attempt at assessing the compliance costs of the retail investment sector (life assurance, pensions and unit trusts) was undertaken by Peacock and Bannock,[3] who concluded that total compliance costs in this sector of the financial services industry fell within the range of £135-296 million in 1994, or between four and nine times the costs of administration. The assumptions which underlie Peacock and Bannock's calculation are explained clearly in their report.[4] It is evident that throughout they have used conservative assumptions. Furthermore, these costs do not include any

---

1   D. Lomax, *London Markets after the Financial Services Act*, London: Butterworth, 1987.

2   Franks and Schaefer, *op.cit.*

3   Peacock and Bannock, *op.cit.*

4   *Ibid.*, pp.37 and 38.

allowance for the cost of the Investors Compensation Scheme nor of the costs of professional indemnity insurance. Nor do they include fines levied on the industry, nor any allowance for the costs of the Recognised Professional Bodies (RPBs). Peacock and Bannock observe that the size of compliance costs in the retail investment business reflects the prescriptive nature of the regulatory system.

3. Excess Burden of Costs

No estimates of the excess burden of regulatory costs have been made for the UK, although some attempted assessments have been made for the United States for other industries such as airlines.

The Burden of Costs

The identifiable costs of regulation (the sum of the costs of administration and the costs of compliance) are estimated by Peacock and Bannock to fall within the range of £169-330 million in the year 1994. Given that the assumptions which underlie these estimates are on the conservative side, and that the estimates themselves pre-date the introduction of product disclosure requirements in 1995 which added significantly to the compliance costs of regulation by lengthening the sales process, then it is possible to take £300 million as an approximate figure for the total regulatory costs borne by the industry. It is instructive to express this as a ratio of total industry turnover in order to compare the burden with that of regulatory costs in other industries and in other countries.

The PIA has suggested[5] that the costs of regulation should be expressed as a proportion of the industry's gross premium income. However, the appropriate figure to measure the turnover of the life assurance industry is not its gross premium income. The gross premium income is simply the annual increment in the funds which it manages. The gross output or turnover of the industry is more correctly identified with the industry's earnings from charges. In 1994 the industry's gross premium income was around £23 billion, and earnings from charges might be taken to be around 15 per cent of that figure. Fifteen per cent of £23 billion is equal to £3·45 billion; £300 million is just under 9 per cent of £3·45 billion. In other words, the measured costs of the regulatory system amount to some 9 per cent of industry turnover.

---

[5] Personal Investment Authority, *Annual Report*, 1995.

The Benefits of Regulation

While costs may be difficult to identify comprehensively, they are, at least in principle, quantifiable. The benefits of regulation of consumer markets are unquantifiable, because they are largely if not wholly subjective. To quantify the benefits of a particular regulation one would need to know, for each consumer and each potential consumer in the market, how his or her purchasing behaviour would have differed in the absence of the regulation, and how much value each would place on the results of his or her hypothetically altered behaviour (including such intangible elements as improved confidence or peace of mind). Supposing each individual could put a monetary value on the benefit thus experienced as a result of the existence of regulation, then a summation of these values over all consumers and potential consumers affected might represent a quantitative estimate of the benefit of that particular regulation.

In practice, attempts to evaluate regulations by a simple calculation of costs and benefits are doomed to fail. Whether the costs of a particular regulation exceed its benefits to consumers must remain a matter of political judgement. But an appraisal of actual experience, and reasoning based upon economic theory, should enter into that judgement.

It is not the purpose of this paper to argue that the measurable costs of regulation have exceeded the measurable benefits. The necessary calculations cannot be made. What we are proposing is that the costs of regulation to consumers would be reduced and the benefits would be increased if the principles upon which the present regulatory régime are based are replaced by new principles, set out in Section VIII below.

What benefits can be claimed for the current regulatory system? Llewellyn argues that the major benefits are threefold: disclosure requirements, training and competence requirements, and the monitoring activities of the regulatory authorities, 'in order to enhance a culture of compliance'.[6] How real are these?

The requirement to disclose charges, commissions and other information to the potential consumer is valuable only

---

[6] D. T. Llewellyn, 'Costs and Benefits of Regulation in Retail Investment Services', paper presented to the Annual Conference of AUTIF, London, 1 November 1995, p.19.

insofar as it promotes more effective competition. In most other markets, regulation would not be necessary in order to secure disclosure of this type of information; we have argued above that it was the absence of effective competition in this market which was responsible for the lack of disclosure.

The idea that the public interest requires the imposition of certain minimum standards of training and competence is generally accepted in other markets (such as medical and legal services) where, as we have noted, the provision of advice is combined with the supply of the service, and where consumers are generally unaware of their own particular needs. That incompetent individuals should be excluded from a market in these circumstances is not in doubt: the question is whether this can be done without unnecessary cost, and without unfairness. The new regulatory requirement that all financial advisers must pass a written test of their knowledge is a step in the right direction.

The benefits to the consumer of the monitoring functions of a regulatory authority depend on what is being monitored, and how efficiently it is being done. If outcomes are being monitored against standards of performance which consumers cannot easily judge for themselves, there are likely to be real benefits. If, on the other hand, as is the case with much of the present regulatory system, it is adherence to prescribed procedures which is being monitored, then it is likely to be of minimal value to consumers and wasteful of resources.

Cost-Benefit Analysis

As we have seen in Section II, neo-classical economic theory offers no practical guide to the nature and extent of regulatory intervention. A pragmatic approach has been to argue that it is important to diagnose the nature and extent of any particular market imperfection and its effects on the price, quality and/or quantity of goods and services being traded in the particular market. One line of reasoning then goes on to say that any decision to intervene by the government must be made in the light of both the costs and benefits of intervention, comparing imperfect markets with imperfect government intervention. Thus, it is said, the next step after identifying a market failure is to carry out a cost-benefit analysis of the proposed corrective action.

The attraction of cost-benefit analysis is that it appears to offer a value-free approach as well as providing quantitative answers to policy questions. It also appears to fit the common-sense intuition that policies ought only to be adopted where their social benefits exceed their costs. However, there are several reasons for being sceptical about the usefulness of cost-benefit analysis, particularly in the area of regulation of consumer markets:

- It is difficult to quantify the benefits of regulation: it is impossible, for example, to measure the effects of the provision of more information or of such intangible benefits as greater confidence in consumer markets since the effect on each consumer is subjective and likely to be different.

- Nearly all cost-benefit analyses of regulation necessarily involve some counter-factual questions – that is, what would be the prices, quantities and qualities of goods or services traded in the absence of regulation. It is impossible to find other than arbitrary answers to such questions.

- Unless one is very careful, hidden and often controversial value judgements enter into the assumptions.

- A concentration on cost-benefit analysis may divert attention from more important issues of the market process, concerning for example the appropriate institutional structure for making decisions affecting consumers.

Many of these difficulties are apparent in the study[7] commissioned by SIB from NERA on the costs and benefits of requiring the suppliers of life assurance contracts to disclose their charges and commission payments.

Perhaps the only redeeming feature of cost-benefit analysis is that it does impose a requirement that the analyst should think through systematically the potential impact of the proposed policy measure.

---

[7] *Costs and Benefits of SIB Proposals to Improve Product and Commission Disclosure in Life Assurance*, London: National Economic Research Associates, April 1994.

VII. THE SUCCESS OF COMPETITION

'We are aiming for an industry that is innovative, vigorously competitive, and peopled by individuals who have a stake in setting, monitoring and maintaining high standards.'

Thus begins a recent policy paper issued by the Consumers' Association.[1] As this passage suggests, the Consumers' Association believes that vigorous competition offers important benefits to consumers. What exactly are these benefits?

Economic theory has several different models of the market.[2] Most of them demonstrate the principle that a competitive market responds to consumer demand in a way which minimises costs. Over time, competition between suppliers should lead to reductions in costs and therefore in prices to consumers, as well as to improvements in the quality, and extensions of the range, of goods and services provided in response to changing consumer demand. Whatever the finer points and differences in emphasis among the different theories, these broad principles have been substantiated by the experience of market economies over the past 250 years. Unfortunately, in economic policy-making as in some textbooks, the responsiveness of competitive markets to consumer demand is often overlooked. Markets can provide solutions to many of the problems identified as justifying regulatory intervention. As we shall see, the onset of a period of more effective competition in the personal investment market has delivered benefits to consumers which regulation seems to have been unable to bring about.

Limited Competition

At the time of the Gower Report, the life and pensions market was wholly insulated from competition from abroad, although

---

[1] *Financial Services Regulation, A Consumer Agenda,* London: The Consumers' Association, June 1996.

[2] See Section II above, pp.16-27.

foreign companies could establish operations in the UK. Within the domestic market, a long history of association with government meant that life insurance companies had developed almost para-statal characteristics. In return for acquiescing in prudential supervision, as in having a company employee (the Appointed Actuary) assume public responsibilities, life companies were granted a number of privileges. One of these was that they were effectively protected from becoming insolvent. Anti-competitive trading practices such as the Maximum Commission Agreement and the lack of transparency in investment contracts were tolerated – even encouraged – by government. All these arrangements can be traced to the paternalistic belief that consumers were too short-sighted to be the best judges of their own interests, a belief encapsulated in the maxim that life insurance is never bought, but must be sold. The result was the development of a non-competitive culture. The very name 'life offices' has non-competitive overtones.

Until the beginning of this decade there was virtually no price competition between suppliers of investment contracts. Indeed, since prices (charges) were not disclosed to consumers, there was no basis for such competition. Competition on product quality was limited by the opacity of the contracts, an arrangement in the interests of the distributors, which thereby gained an opportunity for selling advice. Another symptom of the low degree of competition was that the industry was slow to develop *good quality* new products to meet emerging customer needs in the areas of home income plans, critical illness and long-term care. Policies tended to be designed by actuaries rather than by marketing people. The use, as a starting point, of common mortality tables, together with a professional bias towards conservative valuation methods may have led to an effective price cartel. The industry was supply- rather than demand-driven.

Thus, in the early 1980s the industry was characterised by weak price competition, high exit barriers and opacity of contract terms, behind which some companies were able to operate with high costs, while those intermediaries which wished to do so were able to sell sometimes unsuitable high-commission products to their clients. The market was crying out for more effective competition.[3] What it got was more regulation. The stance of official policy towards competition in the personal investment market in the mid-1980s ranged from indifferent to hostile. Concerns then expressed by the OFT about the anti-competitive character of some of the new regulations were brushed aside by the government of the day.

The Government's apparent indifference towards effective competition in the personal investment market has been in marked contrast to its attitude towards competition in the wholesale financial markets. Here, the Treasury has always pushed for maximum deregulation, being an enthusiastic supporter of light regulation within the City, the Single Passport and Big Bang.[4] When it came to retail markets, however, the Government's enthusiasm for the efficacy of competition seems to have evaporated. Its response to early revelations of misconduct in the retail market was to move in the opposite direction, away from competition and towards increased regulation. Two explanations for these conflicting attitudes are possible.

First, the Treasury appears to take a mercantilist view of regulatory policy; its primary motive in urging de-regulation on the wholesale financial markets was in order to safeguard the City of London's international competitive position. This suggests that when the personal investment market becomes open to foreign competition, the industry may no longer have to put up with the Financial Services Act (see Section IX below).

The *second* explanation is that while consumers in wholesale markets were deemed to be able to look after themselves, government believed that ordinary households would be unable to cope with a truly competitive market for personal investment, and needed to be protected by a highly restrictive régime of regulation. It seems that government did not have a high opinion of the industry as they saw it in the early 1980s,

---

[3] 'Furthermore, it is evident that sellers of financial services are competing less on price and quality, as in traditional markets, but more on the methods of sale and promotion – which makes it particularly hard for investors to compare products.' (House of Commons Treasury and Civil Service Committee, HC 332, *op.cit.*)

[4] 'Changes in the Stock Exchange and Regulation of the City', *Bank of England Quarterly Bulletin*, Vol. 27, No. 1, February 1987.

but it seems equally clear in retrospect that that response was wrong.

Effective Competition

Subsequently, from around 1990, there was a significant intensification of competition within the industry. This did not come about as a result of government policy, but as a result of the entrance of new suppliers into the industry, principally bancassurers and others providing substitute products, together with the development of new telephone-selling technologies. The introduction, from 1 January 1995, of an obligation on companies to disclose at the point of sale the level of charges and commissions paid to the selling agent has not always led to a reduction in the complexity of pricing structures. It is as a result of greater price competition in the market that the transparency of contract terms has increased, firms have felt under pressure to lower their costs, and some hitherto complex contracts have been made more simple by unbundling, thus ending previously disguised cross-subsidies.

One of the consequences of this increased competition has been the further evolution of corporate branding, encouraging customers to identify trustworthy providers. Branding has been emphasised in particular by such new entrants as Marks & Spencer, Direct Line and Virgin. Branding is a natural response of competitive markets to the customer need for confidence. Today, few would doubt the intensity of competition within the industry.[5] Intensified competition has benefited consumers through cost reductions and through the development of new products, as well as by adding to their confidence through branding.

Competition could be further intensified, and the choice of consumers further extended, by the removal of existing barriers to international trade in life assurance and pensions products. Within the European Union, these barriers have been lowered but not eliminated by the coming into operation

---

[5]   There may, however, be a legitimate concern about the influence of regulation in bringing about an undue concentration of market power in the hands of a few groups of Independent Financial Advisers. This is something the OFT might examine. There is also a danger of 'presentational' competition – that is, of competition taking place on the basis of the data required to be disclosed.

of the Single Market in July 1994, since significant tax barriers remain.[6]

The effects of price competition can be looked at under four headings: the effects on charges, on customer service, on mis-selling and on the commission paid to intermediaries.

Falling Prices

While there is an acute scarcity of comprehensive and comparable data on charges (prices) for the industry as a whole, there would be general agreement within the industry that the intensified competition which has appeared since the early 1990s has been the principal contributor to the decline in charges across a wide range of products. This has become particularly apparent since the disclosure of charges was required from 1 January 1995.[7]

Unit trusts are substitutes for many other investment products. In 1995, Virgin launched an index-tracking PEP with no entry or exit charges and an annual management charge of 1 per cent, below the then prevailing industry average. Other competitors followed suit, with the result that overall charges in the PEP unit trust market have fallen over the past two years. Front-end charges have almost disappeared.

Service

Since investment contracts last for a number of years, service (the administration of premium collection, fund management and payment of claims) is an important ingredient of the product. While it is impossible to quantify, there would again be general agreement in the industry to the proposition that increased competition has led to a significant improvement in the average levels of service offered to customers.

---

[6]   As a consequence of a 1992 Judgement of the European Court, the Bachmann Judgement, which unexpectedly legitimised discrimination between member-states in the taxation of cross-border life assurance services.

[7]   For example, the journal *Money Management* conducted surveys in July 1994 and July 1995 of unit-linked personal pensions. These surveys covered some 60 companies. On a 25-year unit linked personal pension, the survey suggested that charges had fallen by an average of 3·2 per cent between these two dates. The reduction was greatest amongst those companies which had the higher charges to start with. The PIA commented: 'This may indicate some efficiency gains which have fed through to customers or increased price competition.' (PIA, *Life Assurance Disclosure: One Year On*, January 1996, p.5.)

Mis-Selling

As explained in Section IV, the ratio of forfeitures to new business provides an indicator of changes in the extent of mis-selling. From Figure 2 (above, p.39) it is apparent that, although forfeiture rates in 1994 were little better than those 10 years' earlier, from about 1991 onwards there appears to have been an improvement in the forfeiture rate. It is impossible to say with conviction whether this improvement is a response to regulation, to increased competition or to other factors. But those who believe that the improvement is a response to regulation would have to explain why there was such a long time-lag between the coming into effect of the new regulatory framework and the improvement in the rate.

Commission

While price competition appears to have had the effect of lowering the prices charged by companies to consumers, that part of the price which is paid as commission to intermediaries does not seem to have fallen. Indeed, it appears to have increased. A survey by the Life Insurance Association in May 1995 indicated that commissions available to Independent Financial Advisers increased in the period between August 1993 and October 1995.[8] Levels of commission paid to IFAs are now around 140 per cent of the level authorised by LAUTRO in 1990. The fact that commission rates have increased in the face of an increase in the general level of price competition indicates that there is a continuing problem which needs to be addressed.

Regulation and Competition

As we have noted, Gower saw an inevitable conflict between competitive market forces and regulation; the adversarial spirit of the regulatory process set up under the Financial Services Act reflects this perceived conflict. Recently, however, a change of tone can be detected in the pronouncements of one of the principal regulatory bodies, the PIA.

For example, a recent discussion paper suggests a willingness to reconsider such a fundamental objective as investor protection:

---

[8] Quoted in PIA, *Life Assurance Disclosure: One Year On, ibid.*, p.12.

'We are now starting to think that "investor protection" as a concept has two unhelpful connotations. One is that it might seem to offer "protection" from risk – which regulators cannot and in our view should not pretend to be able to do. The second is that it seems to imply that buyers need "protection" from the sellers in this marketplace – an idea which is hardly calculated to encourage people to carry out transactions that are hugely important for themselves and their families.' [9]

While this change of attitude is to be welcomed, it is too early to say whether it will lead to a significant change in regulatory practice. There have been some incremental improvements, such as a truncation of the prescribed sales process. The fact remains that the present framework of regulation remains fundamentally unsound. It leaves scope for arbitrary and inconsistent behaviour, and for an absence of responsibility when things go wrong.

---

[9] 'Evolution Project', PIA Discussion Paper, London: Personal Investment Authority, September 1996, p. 4.

VIII. NEW PRINCIPLES OF REGULATION

Objectives

The objective of regulation should be restated as being the creation of a market within which all consumers can deal with confidence.

This formulation has a number of advantages over the old objective of 'investor protection'. *First*, it recognises the central rôle played by the market in satisfying consumer needs, and implies that regulators should reinforce market forces rather than work against them. *Second*, it rejects the paternalistic implications of the phrase 'investor protection' and recognises instead that the ultimate responsibility for the purchasing decision cannot be taken from the consumer.

However, if a market is to perform its functions adequately, consumers must have full confidence in it. This confidence will be engendered by trust in suppliers, supported by a belief in the rules of the market, formal and informal. Fair trading practices must prevail.

In recent months there has been an encouraging shift in statements by regulators about the objectives of regulation. More recognition has been given to the importance of competition as the principal means of protecting consumer interests. If they are to carry conviction, these words must be backed up by deeds. Methods of regulation and the institutional structure of regulation must change accordingly.

Methods of Regulation

How is the objective of creating a market in which all consumers can deal with confidence to be realised? The answer must be by promoting vigorous competition accompanied by the effective enforcement of laws against fraud and unfair trading.

As we saw in the last section, the Consumers' Association is a strong believer in the benefits to the consumer which vigorous competition can bring, not least through innovation. And at least one regulator believes that competition is more effective than regulation in encouraging efficiency and stimulating innovation:

> 'Competition frequently surprises through the rapidity of change which it produces. Consequently, the best policy for a regulator in this kind of field is to focus on helping markets to work more effectively, and on removing impediments to competition.'[1]

Competition should replace prescriptive regulation as the means of raising standards of conduct within the industry. Most financial businesses know that probity is important to their success. They have internal discipline and standards. The danger of regulation by procedural rules is that it can generate the opposite kind of culture. 'It's all right if we can get away with it' can replace 'Our reputation is at stake'. It externalises the discipline, laying off the task of being honest to an outside inspector. In general, a reputation for trustworthiness is a competitive asset in the personal investment market. Effective competition is likely to promote integrity more than any ethics committee or any amount of rules about training and competence.

How to Control Bad Advice

If confidence is to be restored to the personal investment market, fair trading laws must address not only the general problems of fraud and theft, but also the problem peculiar to that market, namely mis-selling or bad advice – the practice of recommending a product which may not be best suited to a customer's needs, but which offers a higher commission to the selling agent (whether employed or self-employed). How can the difficulties facing the consumer in trying to make an informed judgement (because of the un-knowability of the investment return, the infrequency of the purchase and the costs of processing the information) be overcome?

Prescriptive regulation is of limited value in these circumstances. Even after the event it will not, in general, be possible to say whether the best contract was recommended; the question of best advice is an unavoidably subjective issue. Only in a small number of cases will it be possible to show unambiguously that bad advice had been offered.

---

[1] Sir Bryan Carsberg, *Annual Report of the Director General of Fair Trading*, London: HMSO, 1992.

In these circumstances of unavoidable subjectivity, the only factor which can be relied upon is trust. The consumer must form a judgement about who constitutes a trustworthy supplier or agent. It is here that corporate branding plays an important rôle in helping the consumer to distinguish between trustworthy and untrustworthy suppliers. This can be done with the aid of the media, or even by word of mouth.

In the longer term, the market can be expected to evolve other solutions to the problem of advice. One such solution is for increasing specialisation to evolve a class of people who will sell financial planning advice to customers independently of the supply of financial products. So far this has not happened on a significant scale; the generality of consumers has proved reluctant to pay for financial advice on a fee-for-service basis. Another is the introduction of knowledge-based computer software to help the consumer with his or her financial planning decisions, avoiding the need to buy advice in all but the most complex circumstances.

In circumstances of effective competition, companies might be expected to compete not only on the investment return, on price and on quality of service but also on quality of advice as well. Regulators could help to stimulate competition on quality of advice by evaluating comparative performance in this respect and by providing well-publicised awards. Other measures which would help to reduce the incidence of bad advice include raising the standards of competence for advisers and improved consumer education (see sub-section headed 'Consumer Education', below, pp.75-76).

However, until such solutions have been more widely adopted, the problem of commission bias may have to be addressed more directly by restoring, as a temporary expedient, a regulatory limit on the rates of commission paid to selling agents, whether independent or company salesmen. Such limits existed in Britain up to 1989, as the result of a series of informal agreements among suppliers within the industry.[2] A similar arrangement prevails in Singapore at the present time, and appears to have contributed to significantly lower rates of mis-selling in that country.[3]

---

[2] The Maximum Commission Agreement (MCA) was abolished in 1989 after being declared anti-competitive by the OFT, which anticipated that full disclosure of charges and commissions to the consumer would render it redundant.

[3] See Mercantile & General Reinsurance…, *op.cit.*, pp.162- 64.

Standards of Conduct

The market behaviour of sellers and their agents should no longer be controlled by prescribing and monitoring detailed and arbitrary procedures. The lessons of attempting to apply prescriptive rules of behaviour in such circumstances in other countries show that they are both costly and ineffective.[4] Instead, the objectives of regulation and the broad principles of its operation should be laid down by statute. Working principles or standards of conduct[5] should be the responsibility of the regulators. Who should set these standards and what might they be?

In other industries, the fairness of trading practices is judged by the Office of Fair Trading (OFT). For example, this body monitors the trading practices of the banks and other financial institutions. Furthermore, the OFT is the government agency principally responsible for competition policy. Hitherto, its influence on the selling practices of the life assurance industry has been mediated through the PIA and the SIB. There is no good reason for these latter two bodies to be involved. In conjunction with industry and consumer representatives, the OFT could set standards of market conduct directly for the life and pensions industry, just as it does for other industries. The other regulatory bodies should be obliged actively to encourage competition, in the same way that utility regulators have pro-competition responsibilities which have been used actively for the benefit of consumers.

In setting standards, it may not be necessary to devise many new rules. Much could be taken from existing legislation, which at present appears to lack enforcement. For example, Section 63 of the Insurance Companies Act 1974 states that any person promising or forecasting misleading information or making any reckless claims or statements in order to induce another person to enter into any contract of insurance (including life assurance) shall be guilty of an offence. This would seem to include the possibility of any company or agent being sued for bad advice.

---

[4] Howard, *op.cit.*

[5] In framing standards of conduct, account should be taken not only of different levels of knowledge amongst consumers – that is, information processing costs – but also the different risk profiles of different classes of contract. Different standards of conduct might apply in the case of selling shares, pensions contracts and bank deposits.

The Trade Descriptions Act 1968 makes it a criminal offence for a false or misleading description to be given to services or goods during the course of trade.

The Misrepresentation Act 1967 says that a person who enters into a contract after a misrepresentation made to him by another party and suffers loss as a result can either rescind the contract or confirm it and then claim damages.[6] This includes innocent and not just fraudulent misrepresentation, unless the person who made it can prove that there were reasonable grounds to believe that the facts represented were true. Fraudulent misrepresentation is a criminal offence under the Financial Services Act. Other relevant legislation which might offer guidance to those drawing up such standards would include the Consumer Credit Act of 1974. This is a market which shares some, but not all, of the characteristics of the personal investment market.

Failure to observe the minimum standards of conduct on the part of a seller (whether company or agent) should lead to the loss of its authorisation to do business. A wilful disregard for minimum standards should be a criminal offence leading to imprisonment for specific individuals. The effectiveness of the SEC as a regulatory authority in the United States is due to fear of the consequences of conviction as well as to the chances of wrongdoing being found out.[7] In the absence of a self-regulatory régime, penalties, whether of a civil or criminal nature, should be a matter for the courts, not for a regulatory body. In effect, the proposal is to replace regulation by supervision. Regulation is about strictly defined rules laying down in detail how consumers should be treated, what information they should receive, and what they can and cannot be sold. With supervision, the law sets a framework within which authorised companies are left to make their own decisions. The authorities may, however, monitor the quality of services offered and the way in which the institution conducts itself in pursuing them. In retail financial services at the present time, the life assurance companies are regulated, whereas the banks are supervised.

---

[6] If the policyholder's ability to sue for bad advice is to be an effective sanction, the selling agent must have the means to pay, which in turn means he must be bonded in some way.

[7] The scope of the SEC's remit does not extend to the marketing of life assurance, the regulation of which is the responsibility of the individual States.

Other Measures

There is a rôle for the regulator in monitoring the market to ensure that the specified standards are met, for example by 'mystery shopping'.[8] In addition, the regulator should make sure that comparative data on charges (prices), investment performance, persistency rates, standard of service and assessments of quality of advice are available.

Disclosure requirements should be extended to oblige a life assurance company to disclose not only its financial strength, but also the sustainability of its bonus structure. This is desirable to protect policyholders from the possibility of 'false trading', where a company deliberately runs down its capital in order to buy market share.

While fraud cannot be eradicated, it could be discouraged by improving the chances of conviction and by imposing more severe penalties. At present, the chances of a fraudster in the personal investment market escaping with little or no punishment are very high. This is an issue which deserves urgent attention.

Organisation of the Regulatory Bodies

In place of the present two-tier structure, there should be a single regulatory body responsible for the marketing of all personal financial services. This would eliminate gaps and overlaps in responsibilities, reduce costs and provide clearer accountability. Its scope should cover the entire retail financial services industry, and competing products should be treated on the same basis. Mortgage lending as well as deposit-based products should be brought within the same regulatory régime. The new body should operate a single clearing house for complaints, in order that consumers can be quickly directed to the appropriate ombudsman or other arbitrator. The operations of the regulator must be transparent, and it must have a clear set of performance indicators for its own operation. The regulator should be entirely independent of the industry, and should be seen to be so. The industry's involvement should come not through formal membership of the organisation, but rather through proper representations by trade bodies and individual organisations. There should be

---

8 That is, where someone is employed to pose as a genuine consumer, and then reports on the transaction.

a greater awareness that those employed in the regulatory bodies and in the civil service have the same motivations as those in the private sector.[9]

While this single-tier authority should be responsible for the marketing of all personal financial services, a separate authority should be responsible for the wholesale financial markets. Other bodies could continue to be responsible for the prudential supervision of the different financial institutions.[10] All these bodies should report to the Treasury.

So far as the regulation of insurance companies is concerned, the existing Insurance Companies Acts give the regulatory authorities power to impose 'fit and proper' criteria on insurance companies and their directors and senior managers. This régime has on the whole worked well, although hitherto these powers have been confined largely to the company's 'production' process.[11] There seems no reason why they should not be extended to the selling process. Authorisation could be withdrawn from those companies which violate minimum standards of market conduct. Such interpretations would be open to challenge in the courts.

So far as agents are concerned, it is desirable that responsibility for their authorisation should be placed on some self-regulatory body, putting them on the same professional basis as doctors and lawyers. Those who are not employed by insurance companies should then continue to be authorised by the new integrated regulatory body. Monitoring of the performance of selling agents would continue to be carried out by the regulators. The important difference is that this monitoring would no longer consist of monitoring

---

[9] According to a report published by the Parliamentary Commissioner for Administration (the Ombudsman) in October 1995, civil servants within the Treasury were involved in almost 1,000 cases of fraud costing £5·3 million during the years from 1991 to 1994. In only a handful of cases were those involved prosecuted. (Quoted in *The Financial Times*, 19 October 1995.)

[10] More detailed proposals for an alternative regulatory structure have been put forward by Dr Michael Taylor in his papers entitled 'Twin Peaks' and 'Peak Practice', both published by the Centre for the Study of Financial Innovation, London, 1996.

[11] Recently, however, there has developed a tendency to sanction individuals for failure to conform to detailed prescriptive procedures (for example, as laid down in DTI Guidance Notes), rather than for violating basic principles of behaviour. This is a move in the wrong direction.

compliance with prescribed procedures, but would consist of responding to reports of breaches of fair trading laws.

No schemes of regulation are foolproof. As a fallback, there should be a scheme of compensation to protect unfortunate, but not imprudent, consumers. So far as the liability of insurance companies is concerned, the Policyholders Protection Act should suffice. There should be separate accounting for the liabilities incurred by the activities of independent agents. If expanded, the Ombudsman Scheme (or Schemes) could provide a low-cost alternative to the courts for resolving disputes.

Consumer Education

There is an important rôle for government in promoting consumer education about financial planning, especially in a context where the welfare state is contracting. This should not be interpreted literally in terms of teaching the arithmetic of compound interest. It is unrealistic to expect more than a handful of people to have either the time or the ability to make a careful appraisal of complex financial products. Rather, consumers should be alerted to their need for financial planning, and taught the ability to distinguish between risky and safe investment contracts, and how to distinguish between responsible and irresponsible providers and selling agents. Above all, they should learn how to identify trustworthy sources of advice in evaluating the technical details of financial products in relation to their own needs and preferences, about which they may also need advice. A small amount of public expenditure in this direction could be expected to have a greater return in terms of social benefit than most other forms of regulatory expenditure. There is no reason why this education should not begin in schools. In the United States, the Insurance Education Foundation supplies a curriculum which teaches the fundamentals of insurance within the context of basic secondary school subjects.

The justification for an educational rôle for government in the personal investment market is twofold. As we have seen, the problem of commission bias is exacerbated in this market by quality uncertainty – that is, the consumer's uncertainty about the *quality* of the information he receives. Along with the other remedies we have proposed, education can help to reduce the incidence of bad advice.

Because of its public good characteristics, information is also likely to be under-provided in a normal market. Without government intervention, a consumer is unlikely to receive a sufficient *quantity* of information. Since information from government is not necessarily unbiased, it would be preferable if the research was publicly funded but carried out by another organisation.

Pensions Reform

Many new proposals have been put forward in the current debate on pensions reform. What underlies this debate is recognition of the need to make funded pension schemes available to a much wider segment of the population. The political will to fund an acceptable level of pensions out of taxation appears to have vanished, while demographic factors threaten the viability of inter-generational transfers through any other types of unfunded schemes.

More than one-third of the population, mostly at the lower end of the income distribution, does not participate in funded schemes at the present time. If the returns on future contributions are not to be reduced by disproportionately large costs of administration, a way must be found to cut these costs. The major reason why pension funds cost more to administer than comparable non-pension investment funds is the complexity of the rules of taxation for pensions. Therefore, a simplified tax régime is a prerequisite for any wider uptake of funded pensions, whatever the particular form of the scheme being recommended.

So far as the regulation of pensions marketing is concerned, it has been proposed (by the Consumers' Association and others) that some products, including pensions, healthcare and long-term care insurance, should meet certain minimum specifications guaranteed by the regulator. As with motor insurance, all such policies would be required to contain a statutory minimum amount of cover, but companies would be free to add on other benefits. The idea is that consumers could rely on those so-called 'safe haven' products to meet their basic financial needs, and they could therefore be subjected to a lighter régime of marketing regulation.

Two difficulties with this idea are, *first,* the uncertainty of the investment return – a truly guaranteed return would be very low – and, *second,* that there remains the problem of identifying the suitability of the product to the individual customer's needs, something which requires advice.

Costs of Regulation

At present, there are no incentives for the regulators to control the costs of regulation, whether these be their own costs of administration or the costs of compliance borne additionally by consumers. Accordingly, a system of compliance costs assessment (*not* cost-benefit analysis) should be introduced, together with incentives designed to encourage regulators to keep the costs of regulation down. One solution might be to introduce a regulatory budget, which would cap the compliance costs that each regulatory body could impose. This would oblige legislators and civil servants to take responsibility for the costs of new regulations, and it would make these costs transparent.

IX. CONCLUSIONS AND RECOMMENDATIONS

Conclusions

This *Hobart Paper* has shown reasons why the next steps in the evolution of the regulatory régime for pensions and other personal investments should include fundamental changes in the objectives and methods of regulation and in its institutional structure.

The objectives of regulation should continue to shift from a perspective which works against market forces towards one which works with them. Specifically, regulation should work to promote a more competitive market, and desist from those activities which hamper competition. The aim should be to help create a market in which consumers can participate with confidence.

The principal justification for regulatory intervention in the market for long-term retail investment products is the existence of consumer uncertainty about product quality. This uncertainty consists of two principal components: uncertainty about the future investment performance of the contract, coupled with uncertainty about the quality of the advice which may be jointly supplied with that contract. The long-term nature of the contract means that the consumer cannot acquire experience either of the quality of the contract or of the advice through repeat purchases. The usefulness of information gathering before the purchase is made is of limited value, since the outcome is unknowable for any of the parties to the transaction. For many consumers, there will also be high costs of information-processing.

Lastly, since entering into a long-term investment contract may account for a large part of a consumer's budget, errors can prove very costly. All of these factors taken together suggest that consumers in the market for long-term personal investment contracts face peculiar if not unique difficulties.

These considerations, however, do not justify the form of regulation which has been adopted to implement the Financial Services Act, namely the attempt to formulate rules

[78]

laying down in detail how customers should be treated, what information they should receive, and what they can or cannot be sold. Such prescriptive regulation may have done more harm to the consumer than good. It has certainly helped to undermine confidence in the operation of the market.

Perhaps the most important function of a competitive market is to continue to evolve solutions for changing as well as for unsatisfied needs, so it is particularly important that the form of regulatory intervention should avoid impeding the market's evolution. Prescriptive forms of regulation are unlikely to avoid this trap. The market is a process which is continuously generating solutions to perceived problems. Thus markets try to compensate for quality uncertainty through insurance, product warranties, trade marks, corporate branding and other types of quality rating. The investment market has also evolved a range of guaranteed contracts, new forms of which may be less costly than the old. So far as the quality of advice is concerned, the investment market has evolved such solutions as life-long relationships of trust.

As the market continues to develop, one would expect to find increasing specialisation, and, with that, the availability of financial advice supplied independently of products on a fee-for-advice basis. Another development, made possible by technology, is the growth of knowledge-based software capable of assessing the financial circumstances of most individuals. However, until these developments are more widely available, and until confidence in the market has been restored, there is a case for the temporary restoration of maximum limits on the commission payable to selling agents. This should help to diminish, in the short term, the incidence of selling unsuitable products.

All markets depend for their successful operation on the existence of rules of fair trading: without such rules, the confidence of participants in the market would be diminished. Like other markets, the personal investment market requires the effective enforcement of a framework of principles within which participants may operate. Many general principles already exist in statute form. Working principles may be devised by agreement between the suppliers, bodies such as the OFT and consumer representatives. Such codes of conduct relating primarily to market outcomes are very different from rules attempting to prescribe market procedures. They should have the sanction of the criminal as well as the civil law, where appropriate. Disputes and questions of interpretation can be settled by recourse to an ombudsman or another arbitration procedure.

Certain groups of consumers may habitually face high information processing costs: for example, low income groups or the elderly. These social and cultural barriers to information processing ought to be taken into account in designing remedies for information failures. While for some people, execution-only business may suffice, for others, efforts by regulators directed at increasing the supply of information may not be effective. A suitable policy response to high processing costs as a cause of market failure might therefore appear to be a product standard, quality certification or form of licensing for some products. For example, it might be thought appropriate for people in some segments of the market who wish to purchase pensions contracts that 'safe haven' products should be available. But these do not resolve the issue of individual suitability, nor can they truly guarantee more than a minimal investment return. The 'public goods' characteristic of information suggests there is a case for regulatory intervention to undertake a general programme of consumer education in the importance of financial planning.

The achievement of higher standards of practice within the industry, including the provision of 'best advice', should be left to the market to deliver. 'Best advice' is indefinable and therefore unenforceable by regulation. It should not be the function of a regulator to act as a management consultant.

Finally, improved accountability could be secured, and the anomalies of the present regulatory system reduced in number, by forming a single regulatory authority for all retail financial services, reporting to the Treasury. The number of formal tiers of regulation would thus be reduced from three to two.

The changes proposed might require primary legislation, which may have a low priority with either of the main political parties. On the other hand, a new Pensions Act might be the catalyst for changes in marketing regulation. However, should Parliament fail to act, deliverance for consumers and suppliers is at hand. As more and more people become accustomed to buying financial services electronically, they will find overseas suppliers eager to meet their needs. (There is a danger that consumers may be led to believe that all providers, whatever their location, are bound to act in the same way.) If British suppliers are not to be placed at a competitive disadvantage, then the methods of regulation will have to change. The competitive position of the personal investment industry in the UK relative to that in other member-states could be significantly weakened if the European Union adopts an approach to financial services regulation which is driven by competition rather than prescription. On the other hand, if the EU régime is to be prescriptive, then the whole of the EU will suffer in competition with non-EU suppliers.

Recommendations

1. The objective of creating a market in which consumers can deal with confidence should replace that of 'investor protection'.

2. Prescriptive regulation of the selling process should be replaced by monitoring the observance of fair trading laws. Responsibility for drawing up such laws, embodying minimum standards of conduct, should lie with the Office of Fair Trading, in conjunction with industry and consumer representatives.

3. A single authority should be established to regulate the marketing of *all* personal financial services. This body should report directly to the Treasury.

4. Other bodies should remain responsible for prudential supervision, and for the regulation of the wholesale markets. These, too, should report to the Treasury.

5. Effective competition should eventually bring about a reduction in the rate of mis-selling through the further development of corporate branding, knowledge-based software and payment for advice. Meanwhile, a regulatory limit should be imposed on the commission of selling agents.

6. Measures need to be taken to improve significantly the chances of conviction and punishment for fraud.

7. The achievement of higher standards of practice within the industry, including the provision of 'best advice', should be left to the market.

[81]

8. The regulatory authority should promote the collection and dissemination in consistent form of market information, including comparative performance indicators.

9. The regulatory authority should have a formal responsibility to foster competition.

10. The Government should promote a programme of consumer education in financial planning and awareness.

QUESTIONS FOR DISCUSSION

1. Why has the Financial Services Act of 1986 failed to protect investors?

2. What are the arguments in favour of regulatory intervention in the personal investment market?

3. What should be the objectives of regulation in the personal investment market?

4. What form of regulation is likely to be the most effective in this market?

5. Should rules be preferred to principles?

6. What are the distinctive characteristics of long-term personal investment products? Are there other products which share these characteristics?

7. Why has intensified competition not led to a reduction in commissions paid to selling agents?

8. How can the risks of commission bias in the life assurance and pensions market best be addressed?

9. How would you set about estimating the costs of a particular system of regulation?

10. Why does the organisational structure of a regulatory system make a difference?

FURTHER READING

Arrow, K. J., *Aspects of the Theory of Risk-Bearing,* Helsinki: Yrjo Jahnsson Foundation, 1965.

Buchanan, J. M., and G. Tullock, *The Calculus of Consent: Logical Foundations of Constitutional Democracy,* Ann Arbor: University of Michigan Press, 1962.

Stretton, J., 'Regulating Life Assurance: Objectives and Machinery', *Economic Affairs,* Vol. 15, No. 2, Spring 1995, pp. 34-36.

Llewellyn, D. T., 'Regulation of Retail Investment Services', *Economic Affairs,* Vol. 15, No. 2, Spring 1995, pp. 12-17.

Stigler, G. J., 'The Theory of Economic Regulation', *Bell Journal of Economics & Management Science,* Vol. 2, No. 1, 1971.

Newmarch, M., 'Investor Protection: Time for A Rethink', Paper Delivered to Staples Inn Actuarial Society, 3 November 1992.

Niskanen, W., *Bureaucracy and Representative Government,* Chicago: Aldine-Atherton, 1971.

Peacock, A. T., *Economic Analysis of Government and Related Themes,* Oxford: Martin Robertson, 1979.

House of Commons, Session 1994/95, Treasury and Civil Service Committee, Sixth Report, *The Regulation of Financial Services in the United Kingdom,* House of Commons Paper 332, October 1995.

SIB, *The Background to Investor Protection,* London: Securities and Investment Board, 1996.

Better Off Out?

BRIAN HINDLEY and MARTIN HOWE

1. A majority of other member states may insist on a 'federalist' agenda for the EU that a British government (of either party) would find unacceptable.

2. If that occurred, the economic costs and benefits of EU membership would be crucial in determining Britain's response.

3. Britain has the effective legal power to secede from the EU: Parliament could terminate the enforceability of Community Law in the British courts. Withdrawal would more likely be by agreement than by a 'messy unilateral break'.

4. Outside the EU, Britain might become a free-standing member of the world trading system, relying on WTO trading rules. More likely there would be some form of free trading relationship with the rest of the EU.

5. Many costs and benefits of EU membership are intangible. For instance, Britain may suffer from excessive EU regulation and from the more effective enforcement of single market and other rules in British courts than elsewhere.

6. An assessment of those costs and benefits which can be quantified suggests the net effect of withdrawal on the British economy would be small – probably less than 1 per cent of GDP. If a special relationship with the rest of the EU were arranged, there might be a small benefit.

7. The major quantifiable cost of EU membership is adherence to the Common Agricultural Policy (CAP). Escape from the CAP would represent a clear gain to Britain.

8. There would be some loss because of the imposition of tariff barriers on UK exports to the EU but, allowing for switching of exports to non-EU countries and other adjustments, it would be small.

9. Some loss of inward foreign direct investment (FDI) might also occur, though Britain's flexible labour markets (rather than EU membership) may be the principal reason for much FDI.

10. There is no foundation for the idea that UK departure from the EU would have 'dire economic consequences'. 'If the EU ...develops along lines that the UK finds unacceptable on fundamental political grounds, fear of adverse economic consequences should not deter a British government from seeking to change the relationship of the UK with the EU or, in the last resort, from leaving the Union.'

ISBN 0-255 36388-5

IEA Occasional Paper No.99

The Institute of Economic Affairs
2 Lord North Street, Westminster
London SW1P 3LB
Telephone and sales: 0171 799 3745
Fax: 0171 799 2137

£9.00
incl. p&p

SHOULD DEVELOPING COUNTRIES HAVE CENTRAL BANKS?

KURT SCHULER

1. Central banking, though now widespread, is a relatively recent phenomenon, especially in developing countries.

2. Rivals to central banking include currency boards, monetary institutes, free banking, and 'dollarisation'.

3. Most economists and policy-makers believe every independent country should have its own central bank so it can conduct an independent monetary policy.

4. This study, for the first time, shows how central banking in developing countries has performed relative to other monetary systems in developing countries and to central banking in developed countries.

5. Measures of economic growth and 'currency quality' (such as inflation rates, periods of high inflation, exchange rates) for 155 countries are analysed to provide performance indicators.

6. The results show clearly that '...central banking in developing countries has performed worse than other monetary systems and worse than central banking in developed countries'.

7. Moreover, these results are robust. Other methods of analysis or classification would be unlikely to change the conclusions.

8. Central banking continues to spread in the developing world mainly because of the consensus in its favour among economists and policy-makers.

9. 'Political opportunism' also plays its part: central banks will '...more readily finance government budget deficits than more rule-based monetary systems'. Furthermore, central banks '...can be formidable political lobbies'.

10. According to this study most developing countries would have been better off importing monetary policy. Some have recently established currency boards: others should follow their example.

ISBN 0-255 36382-6   Research Monograph 52   **£11.00**
incl. p&p

THE INSTITUTE OF ECONOMIC AFFAIRS
2 Lord North Street, Westminster
London SW1P 3LB
Telephone: 0171 799 3745
Fax: 0171 799 2137

Re-Privatising Welfare:
After the Lost Century

There is now widespread recognition of the difficulties of continuing with state monopolies of 'welfare provision'. Hence evidence is being sought on the possible benefits of private provision of education, medical care, housing, pensions and unemployment insurance.

In this volume, edited by Arthur Seldon who has been responsible for much of the IEA's pioneering work in the welfare field, 10 authors use counterfactual analysis to explore the development of private welfare provision before the state takeover in the late 19th century. They assess what might have happened without that takeover, and draw lessons for the future. Seldon concludes that the 'market process' in welfare is likely to replace the 'political process' so that the state will no longer prevent the market from '...discovering the imperfections of the welfare state and the remedies'.

Contents

ISBN 0-255 36384-2

IEA Readings 45

The Institute of Economic Affairs
2 Lord North Street, Westminster
London SW1P 3LB
Telephone and sales: 0171 799 3745
Fax: 0171 799 2137

£11.00
incl. p&p